NO GRID
SURVIVAL
PROJECTS

ESSENTIAL DIY PROJECTS
FOR WHEN THE GRID GOES DOWN

SOPHIA HALL
RUSTY MATTHEWS

Get Your Self-Sufficiency Checklist

It comes with:
- **A quickstart checklist** — Things that you can do almost immediately that will reduce your reliance on others.
- **A skills checklist** — Valuable skills that you should start learning yesterday!
- **And more** in-depth checklists about topics such as: food, water, energy, waste management, and more.

To get it for free, visit:

www.easygreenguides.com/checklist

Contents

Introduction

Disasters can happen anywhere and at any time. The disruption they cause in your everyday life may be anything from a short-term inconvenience to a long-term survival situation. You're reading this book because you realize life is uncertain and anything can happen. I wrote this project-based book to help you survive and thrive in a no-grid situation.

You have the instinct and desire to protect yourself and your loved ones as best as you can with the resources you have at your disposal. This book is one such resource, and it will provide you with potentially life-saving projects that you can lean on when the grocery stores are barren, or the lights won't turn on.

Disasters tend to beget more disasters, and things tend to worsen before they get better. Just when you thought the coast was clear with covid, you now have to deal with the aftermath. Supply chain disruptions, shortages, market crashes, hyperinflation, and the list of economic woes continue to this day, at least at the time of this writing.

The assumption that you live in an infallible and unshakeable society with systems and institutions that will always function well is not an objective fact. I've learned that just because I live in the first world doesn't guarantee anything. Great empires have fallen throughout history; it's what they do. If history has taught us anything, it's the only consistent one.

This brings me to the purpose of this book. This book details projects to help you survive and thrive in a no-grid SHTF situation. Hopefully, you'll never have to use them, but it's always better to be prepared and ready than to get caught with your pants down, so to speak. But before we dive in, I have to mention a few points on mindset because that ultimately can determine more than the supplies you have stocked.

Responsibility

Responsibility is taking ownership of one's situation regardless of the circumstances and recognizing that you are in charge. You are the captain of the ship, and being responsible means steering the wheel with conviction. Responsibility is understanding that if the ship sinks, then at least you were the one behind the wheel, and you did not delegate the task of your own survival to someone else. It is having ownership of your own life and accepting accountability for it.

Belief In Self

Cultivating a belief in oneself is essential for the survival mindset. Without it, you will be second-guessing every decision. Trust that you will overcome any situation and possess the qualities to overcome adversity.

Understand your strengths and weaknesses. Recognize that we all have limitations, learn yours, and accept them. The sooner you do this, the faster you will discover how to overcome them.

Decisiveness

Making decisions becomes a less anxiety-inducing process when you believe in yourself. When faced with a crisis, one must always be ready to take action. We must make decisions and stand by them.

You will only sometimes make the best decisions, and mistakes and failures will happen. This is what it means to be a human. However, do not dwell on your failures; only look back to learn from your mistakes and keep moving forward.

Adaptability

Bruce Lee once famously said: "Be like water." Water is formless and molds itself to any container. To survive, you must learn to go with the flow of things. Changing directions whenever necessary, growing, and adapting to any emerging situation. When it comes to survival, a rigid and stubborn mind will not serve you. Rather, an open mind that can easily adjust to change is much better suited to overcome a crisis.

Situational Awareness

Most people severely lack focus. This may be due to our fast-paced way of life that is filled with distractions. Many are addicted to their smartphones, faces glued to screens with little consideration for their surrounding environment. These habits of modern life need to be kicked in times of crisis, and it is better to practice situational awareness sooner rather than later.

Resilience

When a crisis happens, how well you adapt to it is determined by your resilience. The less time you spend in fear, denial, and despair, the sooner you begin plotting your next move. Resilient people do not give up, which helps them avoid wasting time on thoughts and emotions that do not serve their purpose of survival.

Now that we have that out of the way, on to the good stuff.

WATER PROJECTS

Water Projects

There's a reason why life emerged on earth. It just so happens that our planet checks all the boxes/conditions for the formation of liquid water. Where you find water, you find life. When scientists search for life outside of earth, they're looking for water.

Normal active humans need at least half a gallon of water daily, at the minimum. Pregnant or nursing women will need more, and so will a person who is ill. You also need water to cook your food and to practice basic hygiene. As a general rule of thumb, it is recommended that you store at least 1 gallon of water per person per day.

In a prolonged disaster, supplies may run low. Food should be rationed, but do not ration your water. It is much better to keep drinking healthy amounts while searching for a new source. Your immediate goal should be to avoid dehydration because, in comparison, starvation is easier to endure.

During a natural disaster, your community may be cut off from all utilities for an unknown time. It is advised to store at least two weeks' worth of water. If you live in an area where you're blessed with rain, you can build your own rainwater harvesting system.

The Rooftop Rainwater Catchment System

Difficulty: Medium

Humans have been collecting and harvesting rainwater for centuries. In theory, this water is safe to consume, assuming you drink it straight from the cloud it fell from. In reality, a system will need to be put in place, allowing you to collect/store rainwater with the least amount of contamination.

Rainwater is typically collected from your roof, diverted into your gutters, and finally collected in a container. While rainwater is clean and safe to consume, the variables involved in collecting it could introduce many ways to contaminate your end product. For instance, if your roof is made of asphalt shingles, you must take additional precautions before consuming rainwater. This is because some asphalt shingles may leak chemicals and particulates that will end up in your water and can be dangerous even if using the water solely for irrigation. If you are in an emergency, don't hesitate, regardless of your roof material. Lack of water will kill you faster than chemicals leaking from the asphalt. Materials like slate, tile, or metal are much better suited for collecting rainwater from your roof.

If your roof is made of an appropriate material, you're not quite off the hook. Roofs can get pretty filthy - dirt, bird droppings, leaves, and other contaminants will also be present. The first few minutes of a downpour will 'clean' your roof and get rid of most of the bad stuff; this does not mean your rainwater is now safe to consume. It simply means that it is less contaminated and is now adequate only for emergencies. To make rainwater collected from your roof safe to consume, you would need to install a reliable filtration system, and you would also have to purify it.

The amount of rainwater you can collect largely depends on the size of your roof and the rain amount in your area (measured in mm/inches using a rain gauge). You can use the following formula to get a rough approximation:

Imperial

$$A \; x \; R \; x \; 0.62 = C$$

A = Roof Surface Area (square feet)

R = Rainfall Amount (inches)

C = Roof Catchment Capacity (gallons)

Metric

$$A \; x \; R = C$$

A = Roof Surface Area (square meters)

R = Rainfall Amount (millimeters)

C = Roof Catchment Capacity (liters)

A 1000-square-foot roof with one inch of rain can net you more than 600 gallons.

With the right materials, anyone can set up their rain catchment system on a reasonable budget. However, ensuring this is legal in your jurisdiction is important. Most states are okay with this, but you're out of luck if you live in Colorado or Utah. It is always best to check beforehand for the most up-to-date regulations in your area.

Tools

- ☐ Tin snips
- ☐ Power drill with drillbits
- ☐ Hole saw bit (same size as the sandwich bung)
- ☐ Hammer
- ☐ Keyhole saw or jigsaw
- ☐ Tape measure
- ☐ Marker

Materials

- ☐ Building with rain gutter system
- ☐ Cinder blocks or bricks
- ☐ Downspout 90° bend piece

- ☐ 55-gallon industrial plastic drum with removable lid and lockband. Make sure it is food grade or safe to hold water in. You don't know what other people used these barrels for, so buy a new one.

☐ Rain barrel screen

☐ Sandwich bung with spigot (The spigot must be able to screw into the bung)

☐ Teflon tape

Procedure

1. Wash the inside of your water barrel with soap and warm water. It may look clean, but I can guarantee there are residual particles from manufacturing/transporting that you don't want in your water supply.

2. Place your barrel next to your downspout. Make sure that the container is on a flat, level surface. You can dig around and use cinderblocks or bricks to help. This is essential for the stability of your water storage system. Use cinderblocks to give your barrel some height off the

ground so you have enough room to use a spigot on the bottom. Give your barrel a shake to ensure it doesn't wobble too much.

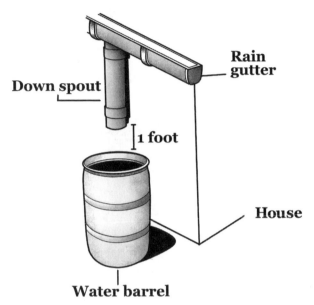

3. Cut/remove pieces of your downspout so it doesn't go down to the ground anymore. Remove parts until you're about 1 foot above the top of your water storage container. If you can't remove pieces by pulling/removing screws, then a pair of tin snips should do the trick.Use the pieces of downspout you removed and the new 90° bend piece to create a nozzle that goes close to the top of the barrel lid. Make the nozzle come out enough to reach the center of the barrel. Leave an inch or two of space between the nozzle and the barrel lid.

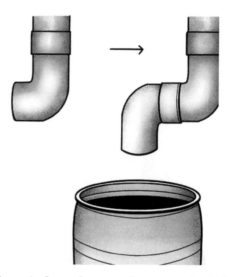

4. Place the rain barrel screen between the lid and nozzle, and draw a circle on the lid. You're going to cut a circle in the lid so you can put the rain barrel screen inside. To cut a hole in the lid, drill a hole in the circle you drew, insert a keyhole saw or a jigsaw, and cut the circle out. Push the rain barrel screen through the hole.

5. Find a spot near the bottom of the barrel and drill a hole for the sandwich bung using the circular saw bit. I recommend leaving an inch or so of the barrel below the hole so sediment doesn't clog the spigot.

6. Wrap the sandwich bung a couple of times with Teflon tape. This will ensure a better seal. Stick the sandwich bung through the hole with the threaded part coming out from the barrel. Use the nut to fix the bung to the barrel and tighten it.

7. Wrap the spigot threads in Teflon tape and screw it into the bung adaptor.

8. Take the remaining plastic shreds out of the barrel, lock the lid on the top using the lock band, and position the barrel, so the screen is directly under the downspout nozzle. Congratulations, you're now ready to harvest rainwater!

This project is one of the simplest ways to start harvesting rainwater without worrying about mosquitos laying eggs in your water supply or sediment buildup. You can modify this build to accommodate a larger water storage tank, like an IBC tote. Also, consider the fact that buildings usually come with multiple downspouts. I recommend collecting rainwater with more barrels from each downspout before moving to larger storage containers.

The water you collect is mostly suitable for irrigation and personal hygiene. In an emergency, drink your collected rainwater only when treated using at least one of the methods discussed below.

How To Safely Store Large Amounts Of Water

Difficulty: Easy

When keeping an emergency supply of water, how you store it matters. While it is generally advised that you have at least a 2-week emergency water supply per person, this requires some space and may not be realistic if you have a large family. At a minimum, keep at least three days worth of water per person. As mentioned earlier, aim to store 1 gallon per person (per day). A three-day supply will equal 12 gallons of water if you are a family of four. A two-week supply would be 56 gallons.

When prepping your emergency water supply, I encourage buying commercially sold water, keeping it sealed and tucked away for when the time calls for it. A common myth is that water expires. You may even notice an expiration date on your bottled water. However, the truth is that the FDA does not require an expiration date for bottled water. Manufacturers stick to expiration dates mainly for stock and quality control. Water will taste better before the expiration date because it has oxygen, which gradually leaks over time and gives water a flat taste. Re-oxygenating your water is very easy; simply pour it repeatedly back and forth between two cups.

While water does not expire, it can still get contaminated with time regardless of whether you have carefully prepared your container and taken measures to prevent this from happening. Therefore, if you do not use commercially bought water and prepare your own supply, replacing your water every six months is good practice.

Commercially available water is great for a short-term emergency supply. It comes in adequate containers to suit that purpose. However, it is better to have containers specifically designed for long-term water storage in a prolonged disaster.

What To Consider When Choosing A Container

Material

Your choice of material for your storage containers should have durability, ease of use, and safety factored in. Refrain from storing water in cardboard containers because these are not designed for long-term storage. Preferably, the material should be opaque because sunlight can cause algae to form. Materials like glass are safe to use but are heavy, prone to breaking, and more susceptible to algae contamination.

Other materials, such as enameled metal, aluminum, and fiberglass, can also be used. However, the king of water storage is plastic because plastic is extremely durable, relatively inexpensive, and light in weight.

Plastic water storage containers are the best for longevity, as you also do not need to worry about rust or corrosion. The only thing to ensure is that you use food-grade plastic because not all plastic containers are equal. Some plastic containers can leak chemicals like BPA into your water over time. You do not want prolonged exposure to BPA-contaminated water, which is why food-grade containers use BPA-free plastics.

Food-grade plastic water containers also come in all shapes/ sizes to suit your specific needs, from the 'grab and go' 2-gallon container to the 55-gallon barrel or drum. You can purchase them from your army surplus or camping supplies store.

Storage

It is very important to make the best out of your prepping supplies area. Save your space by storing things correctly. Use it wisely by purchasing the right containers. Many food-grade containers come in a stackable form factor, which is a great way to make the most out of limited storage space. These usually come in interlocking shapes designed to withstand the load of being stacked on top of each other. They may also come in a brick shape to suit the same purpose. While most water storage containers come in that characteristic blue opaque color to prevent sunlight from forming things like algae, keeping your water in a cool dark place such as a basement or tucked away in a cupboard is advised. If you do not have access to ideal storage space, covering your containers with dark plastic sheeting can help block light from seeping through.

Store your water in a flat and level location. If you have large barrels stored in your basement, put some cardboard or palettes between them and your cement floors because some chemicals in the concrete can leech through the bottom and contaminate your water over time.

Preparing And Filling Your Containers

Always clean your container thoroughly before storing your water. This removes any contaminants that may infiltrate and spread through your supply and ensure it remains fresh/drinkable directly from the stockpile. If you do not adequately clean your container and it gets contaminated, you may need to waste precious energy or resources to treat it before consumption.

Clean your container with dishwashing soap and ensure that no residual soap is left behind when you're done. Use clean water to rinse it thoroughly. Chlorine is also an excellent sanitizing agent, and a teaspoon of it mixed with a quarter gallon of water can decontaminate your plastic containers. Simply make enough of this solution to adequately reach all surfaces of the container as you swish it around. Use clean water to rinse afterward. Household chlorine bleach with 5-9% sodium hypochlorite is recommended for sanitizing your container.

If the water that comes into your house is already treated with chlorine, it is safe to drink and store away. However, if your water supply is untreated and comes from a borehole or well, you must treat it first. Two drops (approximately ⅛ of a teaspoon) of unscented chlorine for every gallon of water is sufficient to eliminate any illness-causing microorganisms. When using bleach to disinfect your drinking water, use a product with a 5.25 - 6% concentration of sodium hypochlorite, and let it sit for a minimum of 30 minutes. The water should have a slight chlorine odor, which indicates that it is safe to drink.

When your container is full, tightly close it and ensure you do not touch the inside of the cap or seal. Always ensure your water is safe to drink and watch out for any odors or floating substances that may indicate contamination. In such cases, or when your emergency supply runs out, you need to know the different ways to treat water and make it safe for consumption.

Pumping Your Water

We already discussed the importance of water when it comes to prepping. Effectively accessing your water in a crisis comes down to choosing the right pumping mechanism. The more water you store, the larger the containers you will need.

If you're keeping drinking water in 55-gallon drums and plan to keep contamination at a minimum, then you will need a drum/barrel pump. Specifically, one that attaches to the container using a bung adapter and can be screwed tightly into the opening of your barrel. Additionally, It should also be long enough to reach the bottom of the drum (approximately 46 inches). A manual pump siphon secured to a tight head drum is the best way to store and access your emergency drinking water without introducing unnecessary contaminants. This pump is essentially a long suction tube with a hand pump at the top, and certain brands give you the option to attach a tube filter at the bottom as an extra line of defense. They are light, portable, and convenient tools to have on hand during a water emergency.

Off-grid preppers or homesteaders considering the option of digging a well/borehole for their water need to consider the type of pump to adopt depending on the depth of the well.

I always recommend rigging a good quality manual arm pump to your well in addition to the typical submersible or jet pump most well owners use. The manual pump ensures you can access your well water despite a power outage. This is less of a concern if your well system/pump is rigged to a solar array. However, having a lever arm pump as a final precaution is always a good idea.

The High-Throughput Water Filter Tower

Difficulty: Easy

It's easy to go out and purchase a manufactured filtration product like the Berkey gravity filter, buy some spare elements, and call it a day. However, knowing how to make your system in a pinch is a valuable skill to have. While a homemade build would not be as effective as a manufactured product, part of being a prepper is knowing what to do if circumstances separate you from your preps and gear.

Materials

- ☐ Two food-grade 5-gallon buckets

- ☐ 20-mm water tap
- ☐ 15-mm tank fitting

- ☐ 15-mm foot valve screen

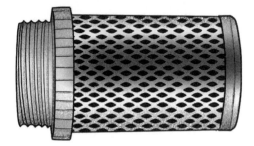

- Four pounds of activated charcoal
- Pebble gravel
- Granular gravel
- Washed sand (play sand)

Tools

- Power drill
- Hole saw bits (22mm and 27mm)
- Round file

Steps

1. Drill a hole using the 27mm hole saw bit where you plan to position the tap. The tap will be a couple of inches from the base of your bottom bucket, receiving the filtered water from the top bucket. Use the round file to smoothen out the edges of the circular hole.

2. Install the tap through the hole. Screw tightly.

3. Use the 22mm hole saw bit to drill another circle in the

middle of your bottom bucket's lid. Again, use the round file to smoothen up any burrs caused by drilling. This hole will channel filtered water from the top bucket.

4. Drill one last hole at the bottom of your top bucket, ensuring that it aligns with the hole on the bottom bucket's lid. An easy way to do this is to flip the top bucket, place the drilled lid on top of it, and drill through the hole which exposes the bottom of your top bucket. Do not forget to finish up with the round file.

5. Install the 15-mm tank fitting to connect the lid and the base of the top bucket. Secure it tightly. The threaded portion should be sticking out the bottom.

6. Screw the 15-mm foot valve into the tank fitting (inside the bucket).

7. You should have a top bucket with a lid attached to its base. Cover your bottom bucket with the lid assembly, and you have a tower. Run some water through the top and test your system for leaks.

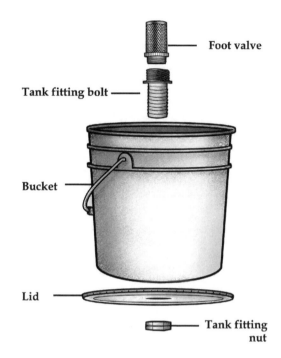

Foot valve

Tank fitting bolt

Bucket

Lid

Tank fitting nut

8. If there are no leaks, we can add the filter mediums. First, we add the pebble gravel, ensuring it is rinsed with water. Rinse until the water becomes clear before adding any of the filter mediums. Add enough pebble gravel to reach the height of the valve filter.

9. The second layer is the granular gravel. Approximately 2-3 inches. Do not forget to rinse before filling.

10. The third layer is the washed sand. Do not be fooled by the label; rinse it thoroughly until you see clear water. Fill it about halfway through the bucket.

11. The fourth layer is 2-3 inches of thoroughly rinsed activated charcoal.

12. Finish it off by adding one last layer of sand, granular

gravel, and pebble gravel on top of the activated charcoal (in that order).

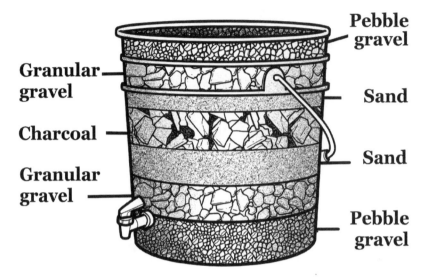

This homemade filter tower can clear up any contaminants from your water. However, if you suspect any viruses or bacteria, it is recommended to boil the water before consumption. This setup is great for clearing up fine debris from your water in a pinch. Keep in mind that it generally takes a couple of uses before the water filter tower reaches its peak filtration efficiency. Allowing the system a 'breaking in' period until it begins to output a water clarity level comparable to your household tap is advised.

Microporous Filters

Many like to make a clear distinction between water filtration and water purification. The distinction is based on the accepted belief that filtration is less effective at getting rid of harmful pathogens than purification. However, filtration technology has come a long way. Several commercially available gravity filters can filter viruses, which are very small compared to bacteria and protozoa.

There are many different filtration systems out there. The most commonly used include gravity filters, straw filters, pump filters, reverse osmosis machines, and water filter bottles. When choosing the right filter, it is important to know how much water it can effectively treat, what kind of contaminants it filters out, and in the case of reverse osmosis machines, energy consumption.

I prefer filtration systems that do not require energy. Gravity filters made by Berkey are highly regarded in the prepping community because of their ability to filter out viruses and their wide range of products. If you're looking for a gravity filter, Berkey probably has one in a size that will fit your specific needs.

Not all gravity filters can filter out viruses, so it is important to know your filter's capability and capacity. Reputable, commercially available filters are the best and easiest ways to treat water during a crisis, and I believe everyone should invest in one. However, it is important to know that a gravity filter will need its element replaced as time passes. Berkey elements will safely filter out 3000 gallons of water until they lose effectiveness. Thus, it is important to have spare elements if you're preparing for a prolonged crisis.

Gravity filters will last longer when used with clear water. Therefore, if your water source is murky or has larger solids floating around, run it through a standard coffee filter before using your gravity filter.

There are many great filtration devices on the market; some brands are better than others. The Lifestraw is an example of an excellent maker of portable filtration straws. I'm not a huge fan of straw filters because many have a limited capacity and take quite the effort to suck. But they can filter upwards of 200 gallons, which can last more than a year for a single person. They are a great tool to have on hand for the low price, especially in a bug-out situation.

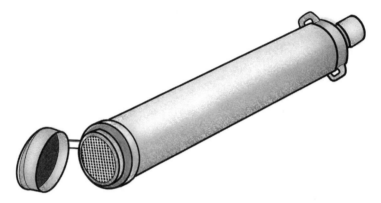

Remember that straw filters are great for blocking bacteria, parasites, and protozoa, but unlike the Berkey gravity filters, they do not filter out viruses. Lastly, a reverse osmosis machine is the only filtration device that can desalinate salt water.

How To Make Water Drinkable

Difficulty: Easy

Do not consume water if you're not certain of its quality because it may contain harmful pathogens. These pathogens can cause diseases such as hepatitis, typhoid, cholera, and dysentery. You do not want to fall ill during a crisis because you may not have access to the medical attention/resources needed to recover. I find that no single water treatment option is perfect, and the best solution in a crisis may usually require a combination of methods.

The most urgent thing to worry about is getting rid of bacteria, protozoa, and viruses. You want to be able to drink your water without ending up bedridden. Other potentially harmful substances (such as heavy metals) may be present in your water, but the microorganisms/pathogens are an immediate threat in the short term. There are several ways to treat water and protect yourself from harmful agents:

Boiling

People have been using this method to purify water for thousands of years. Generally, 5-10 minutes of boiling eliminates the most harmful organisms in your water. Boiling is one of the safest and most reliable ways to ensure water is safe for consumption. However, some water will evaporate, which might not be ideal when your supply is limited. Also, boiling water requires energy, which may also be scarce.

Certain parabolic mirrors/cookers utilize the sun's energy to produce heat. These can be used to cook and boil your water in times of crisis, and they work very well if you live in an area with enough sunlight.

Chemical treatment

As mentioned before, chemicals like household bleach can kill the harmful stuff that may be floating around in your water (remember to use unscented bleach with 5.25 - 6% sodium hypochlorite). Other common household chemicals, like iodine, can also serve the same purpose, and five drops of iodine per quarter gallon are effective. Iodine has a nasty aftertaste, and I generally would not recommend it. Still, it will treat water of uncertain quality if you let the mixture sit for a minimum of 30 min.

Bleach loses its effectiveness over time. A more popular chemical in the prepping community is pool shock, which can remain viable for decades. Pool shock contains calcium hypochlorite, and one teaspoon of this powdered chemical mixed with two gallons of water will create a chlorine solution that disinfects your water. I advise a ratio of 1 part solution to 100 parts of water or a pint of solution per 12.5 gallons of water.

I recommend pool shock with 65% calcium hypochlorite. The best part about using pool shock is that it allows you to make chlorine when you need it without worrying about shelf life. One pound of pool shock can disinfect 10,000 gallons of drinking water if stored and rationed well. If we're dealing with an apocalypse-level disaster, pool shock is a critical item to have on hand.

Ultraviolet Light

There are great products in the market that utilize ultraviolet rays to purify and eliminate harmful organisms from your water. In theory, with enough energy, you can use this method indefinitely. These kinds of products come in many different form factors; they may be embedded into the cap of a water bottle or can look like a stand-alone pen. I find it one of the most convenient and portable ways to have a water purifier on the go. However, this method works best on water that is already clear because the light is not as effective when used on cloudy or murky water. Therefore, you may need to pre-filter murky water before exposing it to ultraviolet light.

Usually, 1-2 minutes of direct ultraviolet light exposure will kill most bacteria, protozoa, and viruses in water, but the correct treatment time depends on the product. Hence, it is important to read the instructions carefully to get the correct treatment time per gallon.

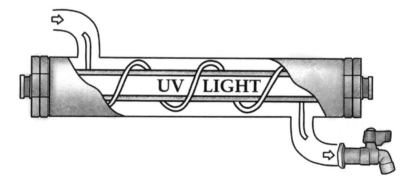

How To Distill Water Quickly With An Energy Source

Difficulty: Easy

This is the process of heating water into steam, which is then cooled and condensed back into the water to be collected into a separate container. This process requires energy, and in a pinch, a makeshift distillation device is easy to make with a little practice. You simply need a heat source, a pot, and a cup. To distill water in an emergency, you can follow the steps below.

Steps

1. Fill the pot halfway with water.

2. Place a cup inside the middle of the pot, and fill it with water, so it remains in place.

3. Place an empty bowl on top of the cup.

4. Cover the pot with the lid upside down, creating a convex shape where the lowest point of the lid is in the middle of the pot.

5. Ensure the collection bowl is not touching the lid or the boiling water and facing upward to catch the condensed droplets from the lid.

6. The steam will rise to the pot's lid and condense back into the cup, making your water safe to drink.

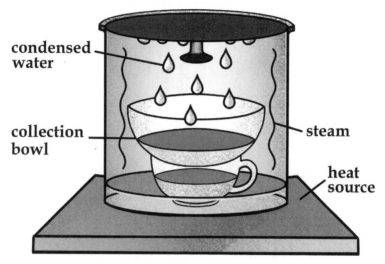

Alternatively, many companies sell household steam distillers that work with electricity. They are much more effective than any makeshift apparatus, and I highly recommend getting one. With solar power, these countertop appliances can be used indefinitely if well maintained.

Keep in mind that distillation removes all the impurities and pathogens in the water, but it also removes the minerals your body may need in the long term. Distilled water is essentially pure H_2O.

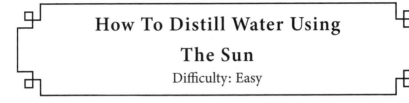

How To Distill Water Using The Sun

Difficulty: Easy

The main disadvantage of distillation is the need for energy, which is never guaranteed in a crisis. However, there are ways to distill your water by tapping into the sun's energy. One such method is outlined below and can purify your water in an emergency, provided there is enough sunlight or the surrounding temperature is high enough to trigger evaporation. Without fuel or electricity, you can still use the pot and the cup we mentioned earlier. However, you will also need clear plastic wrap, a rubber band, and a few pennies this time.

Steps

1. Place the cup inside the center of the pot and pour water, ensuring the water surrounds the cup but is not high enough to spill in.

2. Cover the top of the pot with clear plastic wrap and use the rubber band to secure it tightly.

3. Place the pennies on top of the plastic sheeting to add some weight and create a small depression at the center of the plastic sheeting covering the pot. A small rock or other weight also works.

4. Place this assemblage in direct sunlight and wait.

5. The water will evaporate into steam and condense on the plastic sheeting. The distilled water will bead down to the depression in the plastic and fall into the cup

Plastic wrap   Stone   Rubber band

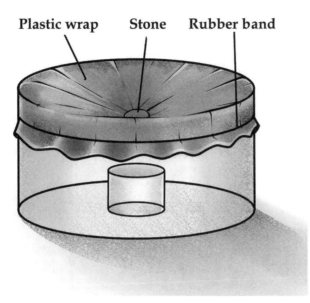

FOOD
PROJECTS

Food Projects

Food is essential for human survival. It provides the energy and nutrients that our bodies need to function properly. In a survival situation, having a reliable source of food can mean the difference between life and death. Preserving food is also important in a because it allows y ou to store food for longer periods of time without it spoiling. Growing food in a survival situation can also be essential. It allows you to have a reliable source of food that you can control and manage.

Canning 101 & Recipes
Difficulty: Medium

Canning is a food preservation method that creates a vacuum seal to keep food fresh and unwanted bacteria out.

Two primary methods to pick from with canning are pressure and water bath canning. While both can be effective when deployed correctly, they are not interchangeable – one will be appropriate for some situations, while the other will be the better pick in some cases.

☐ Pressure canning. As the name would suggest, pressure canning is a technique that utilizes pressure to kill bacteria and keep food safe to eat for an extended period. The pressure, in this case, comes from steam – as the jars are heated, steam pressure builds up in the canner. The resulting extreme temperatures inside the jars kill off any nasty bacteria that threaten to cause trouble down the line. Then, through the cooling process, a vacuum seal is created between the lid and the jar, meaning bacteria won't be able to get in and start to grow while the jars are stored at room temperature. In the end, it's a brilliant method for preserving food and is especially effective for handling foods that are naturally low in acid content and vulnerable to bacteria growth.

☐ Water bath canning. Without a doubt, water bath canning is the easier of the two canning methods. You don't have to create a pressurized environment for your jars, and you might be able to get started with equipment you already have in your kitchen. The idea here is simply to put foods into jars, place them in water, and boil them until the jars seal. While water bath canning is simple, it is not suitable for all foods. Only foods that naturally have high acidity are suitable for the water bath method. Since the preservation is not as powerful with water bath canning as it is with pressure canning, low-acid foods will not be suitably protected for an extended period on the shelf at room temperature.

Foods that fall into the high-acid territory include many different types of fruits. Peaches are certainly one of the most popular options for canning, as they are only ripe for a short period during each calendar year. Instead of restricting your peach consumption to that short time when they are good, you can buy (or grow) a bunch of them and save as many as possible in jars for the winter ahead. Beyond peaches, other fruits excellent for water bath canning include pears, plums, cherries, and berries.

Another common target for water bath canning is tomato sauce. If you love to make homemade tomato sauce for spaghetti and other dishes, you can take the time to make a big batch and then put portions into jars for preservation. Since tomatoes have significant acid content, this is a good pick for those using a water bath to jar their foods. Once done, you'll have a collection of tomato sauce jars on your shelf that you can pull down and put into action anytime a quick but delicious dinner is required.

So, with so many foods making a great fit for water bath canning, what is left for pressure canning to handle? Plenty. The list below is far from exhaustive, but it does cover many of the common targets for a pressure canner:

☐ Many vegetables contain a far lower acid content than fruits, so they must be pressure canned to be preserved properly. It's possible to can all different kinds of potatoes, green beans, and many more vegetables with the right technique and a little practice.

☐ Meats – that's right, it's possible to can meats and keep them safe for later consumption. Of course, the meat will need to be portioned correctly to fit into your jars, but pressure canning is a suitable way to preserve safe and tasty meat options throughout the year. Pressure canning is a particularly popular option for hunters who hunt their own meat and wind up with a bunch of it on their hands all at once. Rather than letting much of it go to waste or having to freeze it all, canning becomes an appealing alternative.

☐ Prepared foods like soups, chilis, and stews are also excellent for pressure canning.

I've included a quick reference table below on what types of food you can can with which method and what foods you can't can.

What You Can Safely Can	
Pressure Canning	Waterbath Canning
Beans	Applesauce
Beef	Berries
Broths	Cherries
Chicken	Jam
Chili	Peaches
Pork	Pears
Soups	Pickles
Vegetables	Tomato sauce

Not Suitable for Canning
Butter
Cheese
Eggs
Flour
Milk
Pasta
Rice

What Equipment Is Needed For Canning?

While canning is not particularly expensive, you will need some basic equipment. In this section, we'll walk you through the basics so that you can be set up for success with your first canning endeavor.

Wide mouth funnel

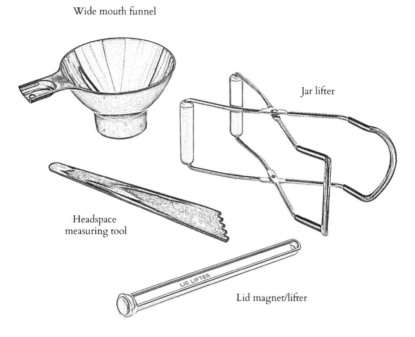

Jar lifter

Headspace measuring tool

LID LIFTER

Lid magnet/lifter

Some basic canning tools

☐ Canner. For pressure canning, you'll want a pressure canner. For water bath canning, any large and deep pot will do.

☐ Canner rack. A metal rack at the bottom of the canner, so the jars are not resting on the hot metal.

☐ Jars. Pick an average size jar for your first batch – 16 ounces (pint) is common – and go from there. As you gain experience, you might find that you like to can larger food items in bigger batches, which will mean you'll need somewhat larger jars. Remember, the jars you use will need to work with the canning equipment you acquire, so that's something to keep in mind as you shop.

☐ Lids. Of course, you aren't going to get far in canning

without lids to cover up those jars. Unlike the jars, which are meant to be used over and over again for years, the lids are disposable. A standard canning lid is meant to be used once before being thrown away. If you try to reuse a standard lid, the seal will not form properly, and your food preservation will not be successful. While the lids themselves need to be disposed of after a single use, the rings that secure the lids can continue to be reused as long as they are in good condition.

- Canning funnel. This simple and affordable piece of equipment will make getting your food into the jars much easier without making a mess.

- Jar lifter. Picking up hot jars using a hot mitt can be awkward and even dangerous if you happen to spill on yourself. Using a jar lifter, which is a set of tongs that have been designed specifically to grab jars, is a much better option.

Elevation

Due to the effect of atmospheric pressure at different elevations, you need to consider where you live when figuring out what pressure will work best for canning. Generally speaking, those who live at higher elevations need to use more pressure in their canner to compensate for the reduced air pressure in the environment. Please check the table on the next page for altitude adjustments for pressure canning.

Pressure Canner Altitude Adjustments		
Altitude (feet)	Dial-gauge Pressure	Weighted-gauge Pressure
0-1,000	11 lb	10 lb
1,001-2,000	11 lb	15 lb
2,001-4,000	12 lb	15 lb
4,001-6,000	13 lb	15 lb
6,001-8,000	14 lb	15 lb
8,001-10,000	15 lb	15 lb

How To Use A Pressure Canner

Between the two, a pressure canner is easily the more intimidating piece of equipment to operate, just because of the potential danger. Anytime you allow pressure to build inside a device, you must be careful that you are following all the necessary safety precautions. That isn't meant to scare you – pressure canning can be performed safely and can lead to outstanding results. Take your time to get to know your device and how it works, and you can look forward to years of safe operation.

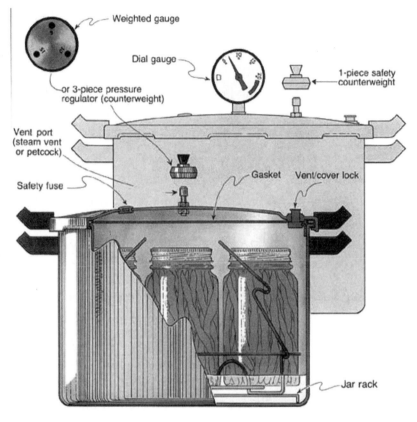

Weighted gauge

Dial gauge

or 3-piece pressure
regulator (counterweight)

1-piece safety
counterweight

Vent port
(steam vent
or petcock)

Safety fuse

Gasket   Vent/cover lock

Jar rack

Using a pressure canner

1. Prepare the food by carefully following the instructions in
    the recipe you've chosen. Of course, you'll need to follow
    standard food safety steps and protocols, just like you
    would when cooking for any other purpose.

2. The canning process itself starts with the task of heating
    your jars. Of course, those jars should be perfectly clean
    before starting to avoid cross-contamination issues. While
    you can heat your jars using another device, it's often
    easiest to do this directly in your canner. Put some water
    in each jar, put some water in the canner, and set the jars

inside. At this point, the lid of the canner won't be locked in place, and you won't be heating the water to boiling. Just get it hot enough to heat the jars and create a steamy environment.

3. With hot jars, begin placing food into the jars one at a time. Be careful not to spill as you fill the jars, and consider using a funnel to make this easier. Once the food is in the jar, and you have left a little head space at the top of the jar, use a spatula or other thin tool to work it around and ensure no air is trapped inside. Throughout this process, work quickly but carefully – you don't want your jars to cool down significantly. At the same time, you also want to avoid making a mess.

4. Before the jars go back into the canner, clean the rims and add your lids. If you use a standard two-piece lid system, drop the lid carefully on top of the jar and then tighten the rings slightly. It is critically important that you do not over-tighten the lids at this point. If you were to tighten the lids down as hard as possible at this stage, you wouldn't be able to squeeze out the air during the canning process, and the whole goal of this exercise will be missed.

5. Once you are done filling your jars and all of them are back in the canner, it's almost time to build the pressure. You'll want to ensure an appropriate amount of water in the canner – about 2 to 3 inches. Now you can lock the lid in place. At this point, the regulator for the steam vent should not be on the unit. You will first crank up the heat and get some steam flowing. This process should proceed for 10 minutes, with the canner venting.

6. After the venting phase, you will build and maintain

pressure for the time indicated by your recipe. It's important to follow timing guidelines precisely when canning, so don't roughly guess how long the jars have been going. Use a timer and track the process carefully to release pressure precisely at the right time.

7. When time is up, the first thing to do is turn off the heat source. Do not immediately unlock the pressure canner and remove the lid. Remember, just because you turned the heat off does not mean all the pressure you created is immediately gone. It will take some time for that pressure to relax, so just kill the heat and wait for a while. Once the safety valve is back down into the unit, or the dial gauge is reading zero, if you have that model, you can carefully open the lid and retrieve your jars.

8. The jars will still be very hot at this stage, so be careful. Using a jar lifter and some protection for your hands, put them somewhere they can cool safely. Once the jars are cooled down, go through them one by one to check for a proper seal. Those that are sealed correctly can go into storage. If any of your jars didn't seal – which will happen from time to time – you should either discard that food or consume it within a safe period over the coming days.

How To Use A Water Bath Canner

Using a water bath canner is less intimidating than a pressure canner, but there is still a learning curve to manage. If you can avoid it, you'd rather not have to deal with any wasted batches while making beginner mistakes that could be avoided with a little bit of education.

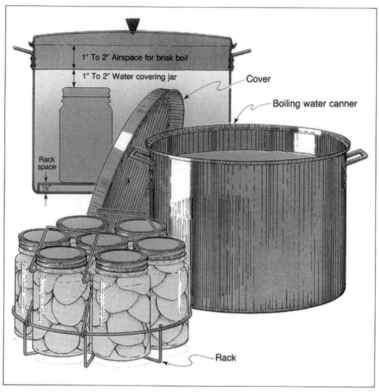

1" To 2" Airspace for brisk boil

1" To 2" Water covering jar

Cover

Boiling water canner

Rack space

Rack

Using a water bath canner

1. As with pressure canning, you'll need to be finished preparing your food before you get started with the water bath canning process.

2. You may or may not need to heat your jars before filling them. Make this decision based on what is recommended by the manufacturer of your chosen products. It is often optional with water bath canning to pre-heat your jars, but always check just to be sure.

3. Since it will take a while to bring a significant amount of water up to temperature, get started heating your water

early in the process. Fill the pot you will use with enough water to completely submerge the jars once they are added. Also, place your jar rack at the bottom of the pot so you have a good landing spot for those jars as they go in. Alternatively, you could load the jars onto a rack outside of the pot and then lower the whole thing into the heated water at one time. That choice is up to you – some people like the simplicity of that method, while others find it a little heavy and hard to manage.

4. The water temperature when your jars go in will depend on whether you are packing your jaws raw or hot – it's 140 degrees Fahrenheit for the former and 180 degrees Fahrenheit for the latter. When you are at that temperature and the jars are ready, you can drop them in carefully. As with pressure canning, you don't want to overtighten the jars – just screw the lids on until they stop spinning under light pressure.

5. With the jars in place, crank up the heat and work to a full boil. You should have a processing time in your recipe that will tell you how long to leave the jars in the boiling water before you are done. Don't make the mistake of starting your timer until the water is officially boiling.

6. Turn the heat off when you have completed the cooking time, and then just let everything sit for a few minutes to cool off. If you have a jar lifter, this is the perfect time to use that toollift the jars out and set them somewhere safe to cool off completely. Again, you'll want to test all the lids after cooling to ensure a quality seal is formed.

The next few pages will cover a couple of general canning recipes that you can extend to other basic foods. These aren't meal-in-a-can recipes; they are geared toward preserving large amounts of simple ingredients.

Fruit Purees

Difficulty: Easy

Water Bath Canning / Pressure Canning

Note: This recipe is not suitable for bananas, dates, figs, Asian pears, tomatoes, cantaloupe and other melons, papaya, persimmons, ripe mango, and coconut. There are no USDA-approved home canning recommendations available for purees of these products.

Directions

1. For any fruits you're using, make sure to thoroughly wash, drain, stem, peel, and remove pits if necessary.

2. In a large saucepan, measure the fruits and crush them slightly if needed.

3. Add 1 cup of hot water for each quart of fruits. Cook slowly until the fruits are soft, stirring frequently to avoid scorching.

4. Puree the fruits through a sieve or food mill. Add sugar to taste (optional).

5. Bring the fruit puree to a boil, or until sugar dissolves (if added).

6. Fill the jars with fruit puree, leaving ¼-inch headspace.

7. Adjust the lids and process as recommended.

Style of Pack	Jar Size	Water Bath Process Time at Altitudes of		
		0-1,000 ft	1,001-6,000	Above 6,000
Hot	Pints or Quarts	15 min	20 min	25 min

Style of Pack	Jar Size	Process Time	Dial-gauge Pressure*	Weighted-gauge Pressure*
Hot	Pints or Quarts	8 min	6 lb	5 lb

* The pressures in this table are for elevations under 1000 ft. If you are at an elevation above 1000 ft, please refer to the Elevation section for an adjustment.

Whole Or Halved Tomatoes (Packed Raw Without Added Liquid)

Difficulty: Easy

Water Bath Canning / Pressure Canning

Quantity: You will need about 21 pounds of tomatoes per canner load of 7 quarts; about 13 pounds per canner load of 9 pints. A bushel weighs 53 pounds and yields 15 to 21 quarts – an average of 3 pounds per quart.

Directions

1. Wash the tomatoes thoroughly, and dip them in boiling water for 30 to 60 seconds or until the skins break. Plunge them into a bowl of cold water to easily slip off the skin. Remove the cores and cut the peeled tomatoes in half or leave them whole.

2. Add bottled lemon juice or citric acid to the jars (refer to the acidification guide).

3. Add 1 teaspoon of salt per quart to the jars (optional).

4. Fill the jars with raw tomatoes, leaving ½-inch headspace. Press the tomatoes until the spaces between them are filled with juice, leaving ½-inch headspace.

5. Adjust the lids and process as recommended.

Style of Pack	Jar Size	Water Bath Process Time at Altitudes of			
		0-1,000 ft	1,001 - 3,000	3,001 - 6,000	Above 6,000
Raw	Pints or Quarts	85 min	90 min	95 min	100 min

Style of Pack	Jar Size	Process Time	Dial-gauge Pressure*	Weighted-gauge Pressure*
Raw	Pints or Quarts	40 min	6 lb	5 lb
		25 min	11 lb	10 lb
		15 min*		15 lb

* The pressures in this table are for elevations under 1000 ft. If you are at an elevation above 1000 ft, please refer to the Elevation section for an adjustment.

Mixed Vegetables

Difficulty: Easy

Pressure Canning

Yield: 7 quarts

Ingredients

- ☐ 6 cups sliced carrots
- ☐ 6 cups cut, whole kernel sweet corn
- ☐ 6 cups cut green beans
- ☐ 6 cups shelled lima beans
- ☐ 4 cups whole or crushed tomatoes
- ☐ 4 cups diced zucchini

Note: This suggested measurement can be adjusted to your liking. You may substitute with your other favorite vegetables except for leafy greens, dried beans, cream-style corn, winter squash, sweet potatoes, broccoli, cauliflower, or cabbage.

Directions

1. For the zucchini, wash, trim, and slice or cube. For all the other vegetables, wash and prepare as described.

2. In a large pot, combine all vegetables and add enough water to cover all the pieces. You may add 1 teaspoon salt per quart to the jar, if desired.

3. Boil for 5 minutes and fill jars with the hot pieces and liquid, leaving 1-inch headspace.

4. Adjust the lids and process as recommended.

Style of Pack	Jar Size	Process Time	Dial-gauge Pressure*	Weighted-gauge Pressure*
Hot	Pints	75 min	11 lb	10 lb
	Quarts	90 min		

* The pressures in this table are for elevations under 1000 ft. If you are at an elevation above 1000 ft, please refer to the Elevation section for an adjustment.

Chicken Or Rabbit

Difficulty: Easy

Pressure Canning

Directions

1. Make sure that the chicken or rabbit is healthy, and must be freshly killed and dressed. For a more flavorful canned chicken, choose healthy large ones instead of fryers.

2. Keep the dressed chicken chilled for 6 to 12 hours before canning. For rabbits, soak it in water with 1 tablespoon of salt per quart for 1 hour, then rinse. Remove any excess fat.

3. Chop the chicken or rabbit into its appropriate size parts for proper fitting into the jars, leaving the required headspace.

4. You can pack the meat with or without the bones. For the best liquid cover and quality during storage, choose the hot pack method. With raw packs, the natural poultry fat and animal juices are usually not enough to cover the meat in the jars.

5. For hot pack: Choose to either boil, steam, or bake the meat until about two-thirds done. You can add 1 teaspoon of salt per quart to the jar (optional). Then, fill the jars with pieces and hot broth, leaving 1¼-inch headspace.

6. For raw pack: Add 1 teaspoon salt per quart to the jar (optional). Then, fill the jars loosely with raw meat pieces,

leaving 1¼-inch headspace. Do not add any liquid.

7. Adjust the lids and process as recommended.

Style of Pack	Jar Size	Process Time	Dial-gauge Pressure*	Weighted-gauge Pressure*
Without Bones: Hot and Raw	Pints	75 min	11 lb	10 lb
	Quarts	90 min		
With Bones: Hot and Raw	Pints	65 min	11 lb	10 lb
	Quarts	75 min		

* The pressures in this table are for elevations under 1000 ft. If you are at an elevation above 1000 ft, please refer to the Elevation section for an adjustment.

Meat Stock, Chicken, Or Turkey Broth

Difficulty: Easy

Pressure Canning

Directions

1. In a large stockpot, place the chicken carcass and add enough water to cover all the bones.

2. Cover the pot and let it simmer for 30 to 45 minutes or until any remaining tidbits of meat on the bones easily fall off.

3. Remove the bones from the pot. Let the broth cool down and discard excess fat. You can remove any remaining meat trimmings still clinging to the bones and add them back to the broth.

4. Reheat the broth to a boiling point, and then fill your jars, leaving 1-inch headspace.

5. Wipe the rims of jars with a damp clean paper towel. Adjust the lids and process as recommended.

Style of Pack	Jar Size	Process Time	Dial-gauge Pressure*	Weighted-gauge Pressure*
Hot	Pints	20 min	11 lb	10 lb
	Quarts	25 min		

* The pressures in this table are for elevations under 1000 ft. If you are at an elevation above 1000 ft, please refer to the Elevation section for an adjustment.

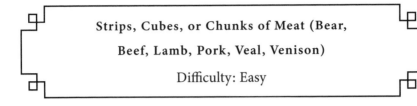

Strips, Cubes, or Chunks of Meat (Bear, Beef, Lamb, Pork, Veal, Venison)

Difficulty: Easy

Pressure Canning

Directions

1. Make sure to use only high-quality chilled meat. Remove any excess fat.

2. If you are using strong-flavored wild meat, soak it in brine water containing 1 tablespoon of salt per quart for 1 hour, then rinse.

3. Remove large bones. For the best liquid cover and quality during storage, choose the hot pack method. With raw packs, the natural amount of fat and juices in today's leaner meat cuts are usually not enough to cover most of the meat in the jars.

4. For hot pack: Choose to either roast, stew, or brown the meat in a small amount of fat until rare. You can add 1 teaspoon of salt per quart to the jar (optional). Then, fill the jars with the meat pieces and boiling broth, meat drippings, water, or tomato juice especially with wild game, leaving 1-inch headspace.

5. For raw pack: Add 2 teaspoons salt per quart to the jar (optional). Then, fill the jars with the raw meat pieces, leaving 1-inch headspace. Do not add any liquid.

6. Adjust the lids and process as recommended.

Style of Pack	Jar Size	Process Time	Dial-gauge Pressure*	Weighted-gauge Pressure*
Hot and Raw	Pints	75 min	11 lb	10 lb
	Quarts	90 min		

The pressures in this table are for elevations under 1000 ft. If you are at an elevation above 1000 ft, please refer to the Elevation section for an adjustment.

Chili Con Carne

Difficulty: Easy

Pressure Canning

Yield: 9 pints

Ingredients

- ☐ 3 cups dried pinto or red kidney beans
- ☐ 5½ cups water
- ☐ 5 tsp salt (separated)
- ☐ 3 lbs ground beef
- ☐ 1½ cups chopped onion
- ☐ 1 cup chopped peppers of your choice (optional)
- ☐ 1 tsp black pepper
- ☐ 3 to 6 tbsp chili powder
- ☐ 2 qts crushed or whole tomatoes

Directions

1. Thoroughly wash the beans and place them in a 2-quart saucepan.

2. Fill the saucepan with cold water up to 2-3 inches above the beans. Let it soak for 12-18 hours. Then, drain and discard the water.

3. Add 5 ½ cups of fresh water and 2 teaspoons of salt to the beans. Bring to a boil.

4. Reduce the heat and let it simmer for 30 minutes. Then, drain and discard the water.

5. In a skillet, brown the ground beef, chopped onions, and peppers (optional). Drain off the fat. Add pepper, chili powder, 3 teaspoons of salt, tomatoes, and the drained cooked beans. Let it simmer for 5 minutes only. Do not let it thicken.

6. Fill the jars with your hot mixture, leaving 1-inch headspace.

7. Adjust the lids and process as recommended.

Style of Pack	Jar Size	Process Time	Dial-gauge Pressure*	Weighted-gauge Pressure*
Hot	Pints	75 min	11 lb	10 lb

The pressures in this table are for elevations under 1000 ft. If you are at an elevation above 1000 ft, please refer to the Elevation section for an adjustment.

How To Make Pemmican, The Indigenous Survival Food

Difficulty: Easy

Pemmican is a survival food that has been around for centuries. The old Inuit tribes of Alaska and some Native American tribes used this recipe on long hunting trips. It is such a nutrient-dense food that many of the first American explorers also began making pemmican during their trade and hunting expeditions.

The concept is straightforward, and basic pemmican can be made with only two ingredients - red meat and fat. When you eat pemmican, you get a healthy dose of macronutrients. Many recipes also add berries, which provide additional vitamins, fiber, and antioxidants. A portion of well-made pemmican can be a fully comprehensive survival food that keeps for decades under the right storage conditions.

There are three main processes involved in making pemmican:

☐ Drying the meat

- ☐ Rendering the fat into tallow
- ☐ Mixing the meat and tallow

Drying The Meat

Traditionally, game meat was used, but nowadays most people use beef:

1. A dehydrator comes in handy at this stage. However, one can also use an oven. First, cut the meat into thin slices, carefully removing the fat. Adding salt helps inhibit the growth of harmful bacteria and enhances the taste.

2. Place the sliced meat into a baking sheet and set the oven to 170F. Heat for at least 15 hrs while regularly opening the oven door to air out the accumulated moisture. The result should be shrunken down crispy slices of meat, which are thoroughly dried out. Do not cut corners at this stage because if the meat isn't dry enough, it will affect the shelf life of your pemmican.

3. Use a meat grinder to crush the dried slices into a powder. Alternatively, a blender or food processor also works. Ensure it is a uniform powder with no large chunks in the mix.

Rendering The Fat

You can purchase ready-made tallow. However, making your own is pretty easy, and the local butcher might even give you the fat for free. Only use fat from beef or lamb when rendering your tallow.

The best type of fat to use is called suet. This fat lines the animal's internal organs rather than the muscles. Ask your butcher for suet because this results in a nutritious tallow full of vitamins and essential oils. Tallow made from regular muscle fat works too, but the good stuff's called suet. Also, remember that tallow made from suet is much harder at room temperature than the one made from muscle fat, giving it a more solid texture.

If you don't end up making pemmican, rendering fat into tallow is still a valuable preservation technique. Tallow ticks many boxes; it is shelf-stable at room temperature, can last up to a year in a sealed container, and is a wonderful ingredient that can add some rich flavors/nutrients to your home-cooked meals. Tallow is a healthier alternative to most vegetable oils sold at the supermarket.

Pork fat or meat is not recommended for pemmican because it may contain harmful pathogens.

To render suet/fat into tallow:

1. Cut off any residual meat from the fat.

2. Cut the fat into small chunks (approximately 1-inch cubes) and place them in a pot with a lid. Every pound of tallow takes approximately 1 hour to render. The pot should be large enough to be filled halfway with the fat you plan to render.

3. You can use the stovetop, slow cooker, or oven. The secret to rendering suet/fat into tallow is to keep the temperature low and cook slowly. If you're using an oven, then keep the temperature at 225F. If you opt for the stovetop or slow cooker, use the lowest heat settings on your unit.

4. It may take several hours to render the fat/suet. Come back periodically and monitor the process while stirring regularly. The fat/suet will dissolve into a nice yellow color, and we want most of it to dissolve into this liquid. The yellow liquid is what we refer to as tallow.

5. Once it's clear that most of the fat has dissolved and the liquid has stopped bubbling, use a mesh strainer to filter the tallow into another pot or container. There will still be brown pieces of floating suet/fat, which the mesh strainer will catch us. You can re-render these last pieces of suet to make even more tallow, but the flavor will be much more 'beefy' this time.

6. The tallow will harden at room temperature, depending on whether you used real suet or regular fat trimmings.

Mixing The Meat And Tallow

Before the tallow hardens, we must mix it with the powdered meat we made earlier. Place the powder in an appropriate pot and pour the liquid tallow slowly while mixing. Use a tray to make a uniformly compressed mold from the mix and refrigerate.

Once hardened, cut into bars, store in mylar bags, and don't forget to toss in an oxygen absorber.

Pemmican is an awesome survival food, but it doesn't taste very good on its own. Consider using dry berries and turning them into a powder using the same process we used for the meat. Any fruit or herb can be dried, powdered, and added to the recipe to enhance the flavor of this amazing survival food.

How To Make Hardtack

Difficulty: Easy

Hardtack bread is one of the oldest, most resilient, cheapest, and easiest survival foods to make. It can last for multiple decades if stored in proper conditions and is a simple way to get a calorie boost when SHTF. It can likely sustain you for a few months if you have nothing but hardtack to eat. Hardtack was an essential component of the rations given to sailors of the British Royal Navy during the 16th, 17th, and 18th centuries. Soldiers and sailors would live off this stuff while out at sea. The recipe is very simple:

Ingredients

- ☐ 2 cups flour
- ☐ ½ teaspoon salt
- ☐ ¾ cup water

Directions

1. Place the two cups of flour into a mixing bowl.

2. Place half a teaspoon of salt and mix with flour.

3. Slowly add water and mix with your hands to make the dough. Make sure it holds together well while being easy to shape. Do not use all the water; we don't want the dough to be spongy like regular bread dough, but also not dry or flaky. If your dough gets too sticky, sprinkle some dry flour to absorb the moisture.

4. Once you have a nice lump of dough, sprinkle some flour on top of your working station. The next step is to flatten the dough using a rolling pin, and the sprinkled flour keeps the dough from sticking to the working surface.

5. Flatten the dough to a quarter inch of thickness. As the name suggests, Hardtack is hard and is difficult to eat when thick. Also, this recipe has no yeast, so the bread will not rise in the oven.

6. You can cut any shape or size biscuit from the rolled-out dough. I recommend making a large square by trimming the edges and then breaking it down into smaller squares. Excess trimmings can be shaped by hand.

7. Use a fork or a chopstick to poke holes in the hardtack squares. The holes help accelerate the release of moisture when baking.

8. Place on a baking or cookie sheet and insert in the oven. The secret to making hardtack is to bake slowly at a low temperature. You will need to bake them at 225F for two hours, flip them, and bake them for another 2 hours.

Hardtack should be properly stored if you want to make it last for decades. Mylar bags and oxygen absorbers are great storage options. Keep in mind that hardtack is almost inedible without some form of softening medium. Consider using it to increase the thickness of your soups or dip it in coffee as soldiers did in the civil war era.

How To Store Dry Food As Long As Possible

Difficulty: Easy

Food buckets

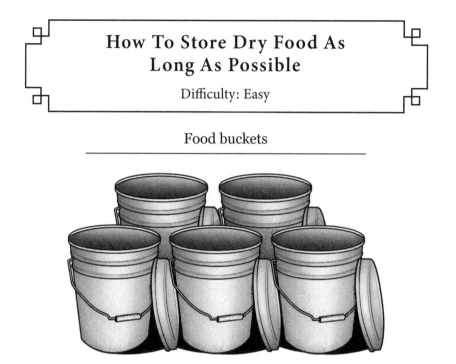

My most used type of container is the 5-gallon food bucket. They are durable, lightweight, food-safe, and airtight. You'll never worry about pests or anything getting past these inexpensive and sturdy vessels.

As mentioned earlier, buying bulk can save you a lot of money as a prepper; this is why having food buckets is so important. If you're buying a 100-pound bag of rice, you don't want to keep it stored in a sack or its original packaging. If you want dry food to last long, you need proper storage containers.

When used with the next item on this list, 5-gallon food buckets are an excellent solution for long-term food preservation.

Mylar bags

Plastic is a porous material (at the microscopic level). You'll need mylar bags to ensure nothing external (even air) can invade your food. This impervious material comes in many sizes. They are suitable for storing food. Also, medicines like antibiotics keep their effectiveness for longer when sealed inside mylar; the same applies to vitamin supplements. Mylar is mostly used when repacking dry goods such as rice, flour, sugar, salt, beans, and pasta.

Most products are not packaged with long-term storage in mind. If you're stocking up in bulk, the best way to protect your dry goods is to line 5-gallon mylar bags inside your 5-gallon food buckets. The bucket will help keep out larger threats such as rodents (keeps water out, too), while the mylar is to prevent more subtle threats like oxidation or light damage.

Smaller mylar bags usually come with zip locks. However, larger bags may require a heat sealer. A hair straightening iron can also do the trick, but you'll need to be careful, so the heat does not burn through your mylar. Ensure the sealed edges are smooth and flat, without any breaks, debris, or particles. Do not fill your bags to the brim. Leave some wiggle room to seal the edges properly.

Before sealing your mylar bag, remember to toss in the next item on this list.

Oxygen absorbers

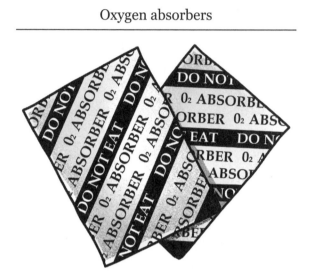

We need oxygen to survive, but so do most bacteria and fungi. Oxygen absorbers are an essential part of your long-term storage supply arsenal. Tossing an oxygen absorber in any type of storage container will extend the life of your food. However, when combined with mylar, this effect is maximized. As mentioned earlier, mylar doesn't let oxygen in as easily as plastic. Tossing an oxygen absorber inside your bag before sealing ensures that the bacteria or fungi don't invade and spoil your food.

Oxygen absorbers have iron powder inside those small sachets, which safely absorb the remaining oxygen in the air after the bag is sealed. It is safe to place oxygen absorbers with dry food; tossing one or two of these bad boys before sealing a mylar bag is one of the easiest ways to preserve dry food for a long time.

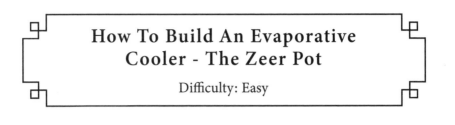

How To Build An Evaporative Cooler - The Zeer Pot

Difficulty: Easy

Our bodies keep us cool through the evaporation of sweat. This project works on the same principle. In this simple setup, we will use water and a few other items to create a homemade evaporative cooler or Zeer pot.

Materials

- ☐ 1 Large unglazed terracotta flower pot
- ☐ 1 Smaller unglazed terracotta flower pot (Large enough to contain what you plan to store but small enough to fit inside the larger pot)
- ☐ Sand

- □ Duct tape

- □ Cotton cloth

- □ A lid for the smaller pot (a regular frying pan lid works)

Tools

- □ Hand shovel

Directions

1. The terracotta pots will each have a hole at their base. Use duct tape to seal them to prevent water from seeping through.

2. Add a layer of sand to the larger pot. The smaller pot will sit on top of this layer. Keep adding sand until the rims of both pots are level.

3. Now that the smaller pot is inside, place the lid on top of the smaller pot to avoid sand from going inside. Fill the gap between the pots until a quarter inch from the top.

4. Pour water slowly and evenly across the sand. Aggressively pouring the water might cause the smaller pot to float above the rim, so take your time. Ensure that the sand is wet.

5. Place the items you want to cool inside the smaller pot, close the lid, and place a damp cotton cloth over the setup.

6. Find a shaded location with proper air circulation to get the best out of your Zeer pot.

This method is still being used extensively in many parts of Africa that have limited access to electricity. Arid places with low humidity tend to get the most value out of a Zeer pot.

During a prolonged crisis, Zeer pots can help preserve fresh produce, provided you have enough water to replenish what gets evaporated. I recommend watering the sand at least twice a day.

How To Build A Solar Dehydrator

Difficulty: Medium

Get your carpentry skills out because it's time to build a solar dehydrator. Even a total novice could build this project if they have the right supplies.

Your typical electric dehydrator is a good investment, but if the grid goes down, electricity may become a valuable resource that you may not want to use carelessly. In this scenario, building a solar dehydrator can help preserve many different fruits and vegetables. Most fresh produce with naturally low water content is suitable for dehydrating using this setup. However, foods such as tomatoes with a higher water content would need an ideal hot summer's day for our solar dehydrator to be effective. Keep in mind that this build is not appropriate for dehydrating meat.

Materials

- ☐ An old rectangular table (The size of your table determines the size of the dehydrator)
- ☐ Hardwood timber planks (Cut to the dimensions of your table)
- ☐ Cover strips or architraves
- ☐ Black paint

- ☐ Corrugated iron (Surface area should be enough to fit snugly on your table)

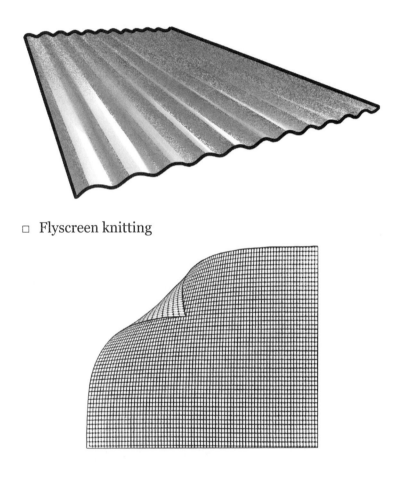

- ☐ Flyscreen knitting

- ☐ Fly screens, framed (Enough to cover the table)
- ☐ A glass or acrylic window frame or cover (the size of your table's surface)
- ☐ A couple of standard hinges
- ☐ Rubber gasket sheet material (optional)
- ☐ Wheels on an axle (kits are available online)
- ☐ Nails or screws

Tools

- ☐ Drill
- ☐ Grinder
- ☐ Clamp
- ☐ Wood stapler or glue
- ☐ Hammer

Directions

1. Cut the hardwood timber planks and position them at the table's edges to create a frame. The table is the base of this build, and the hardwood timber planks must be attached at the corners.

2. Use the clamp to secure the hardwood timber planks to the table. Secure them in place using the appropriate nails or screws. I recommend galvanized screws in conjunction with the drill. You now have the frame of your solar dehydrator.

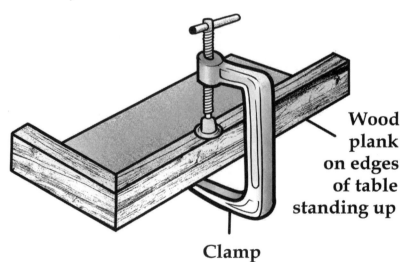

Wood plank on edges of table standing up

Clamp

3. Once the frame is tightly fastened to the table with screws, it is time to add the cover strips or architraves along the hardwood planks' length (longer sides). They should be placed against the inside of the frame and nailed to their respective hardwood planks. This new rail will be the drying platform.

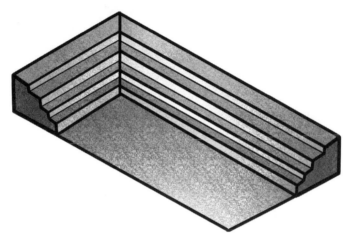

4. Cut the corrugated iron sheets with the grinder, so they fit snugly within the frame and underneath the cover strips (or architraves). There is no need to fasten your corrugated iron to the table or frame; this makes cleaning easier in the long term.

5. Cut your flyscreens to fit when placed on the rail. If you're using old flyscreens, consider replacing the netting because you will be placing sliced fruits/vegetables on them.

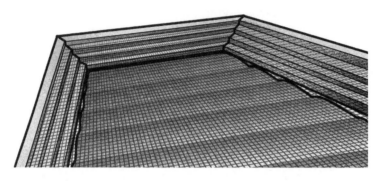

6. Drill a few ventilation holes along the hardwood plank frame's width (shorter side); do this on one side only (half-inch drill bit recommended). Keep in mind that while heat is important, so is proper airflow. Without proper aeration, the humidity will build up inside the solar dehydrator as the water in your food evaporates.

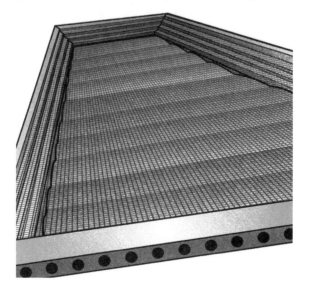

7. Staple some flyscreen knitting to cover the ventilation holes. You may use glue if you don't have a staple gun.

8. Use the standard hinges along the width of the frame (the same side we drilled our ventilation holes) to attach the glass/acrylic window to the hardwood plank frame. If you're using glass, pre-drill the holes (for your hinges) before placing the frame on the hardwood planks. This helps avoid accidents that may shatter the glass while you fasten the hinges.

9. After applying the hinges, you have a cover that opens and closes. Adding a rubber gasket sheeting between the cover and frame helps seal the dehydrator. Unless you feel that there is too much space between them, you can skip this step. However, we don't want flies or insects inside the solar dehydrator.

10. It is time to install the axle and wheels for mobility. Solar dehydrators need to be portable to be placed wherever the sun goes. The wheels will be placed at the bottom of the table's legs, underneath the side where we made the ventilation holes. Use the drill on both legs to run the axle between them, then secure your wheels.

11. A solar dehydrator must have a slight incline for the heat to rise out of the ventilation holes. This means you will need to cut the front legs of the table down. Use a grinder to cut approximately half of the front legs off.

12. Paint your corrugated iron and the rest of the table (except the glass) with black paint for the system to trap and radiate even more heat.

Remember to cut your fruits or vegetables into thinly sliced pieces before placing them inside the solar dehydrator.

A diagram of the complete build is shown on the following page.

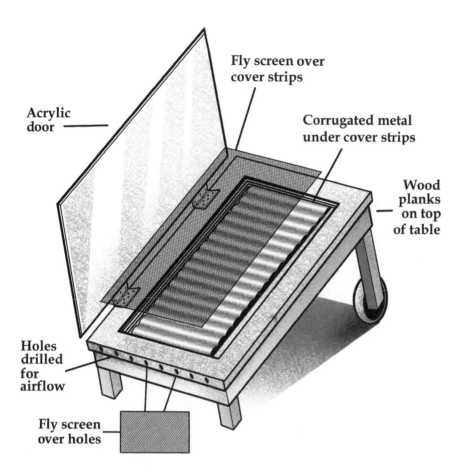

Acrylic
door

Fly screen over
cover strips

Corrugated metal
under cover strips

Wood
planks
on top
of table

Holes
drilled
for
airflow

Fly screen
over holes

Foraging Your Way To A Full Stomach

You'd be surprised at the number of mushrooms, plants, and berries that are edible in the wild, all for the bargain price of 0 dollars. However, foraging is a double-edged sword because what you may think is packed with nutrients may be packed with toxins, which will either get you very sick or worse, dead.

Similar to hunting and fishing, foraging the right way needs a solid investment in time/practice. You'll also need a high-quality field guide for your specific area or state (Preferably one with high-quality photos).

Foraging is a science that works using certainties. Never consume any wild plants, mushrooms, or berries that you haven't 100% identified. Having a good field guide is so important for cross-referencing any wild food down to the smallest detail. Even if you don't plan to start foraging your food, buy a field guide because that wealth of information might not be readily available in a crisis.

There are 100s of edible foods in the wild, even urban parks have plants you can safely eat. However, be careful where you forage because even if a specimen is confirmed edible doesn't mean the coast is clear. Do not forage near areas exposed to chemicals from car exhausts, herbicides, or any sort of industrial contamination.

Universal Edibility Test

Foraging safely needs a good field guide and a lot of experience. However, in a wilderness survival situation where your options are limited, and your food supply is ending, then you may have no choice but to take your chances on a mushroom, plant, or berry you suspect is edible.

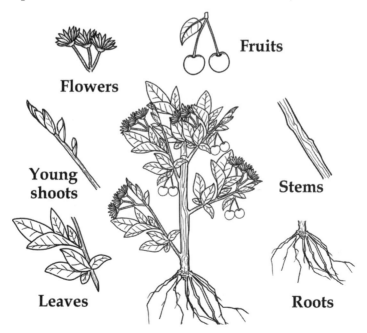

If you're at the end of your ropes, there is a way to test whether a specimen is edible, but you'll have to be a smart guinea pig about it. Remember that the universal edibility test should only be done in a real desperate scenario, and below are the basic steps:

1. Separate the specimen into its parts and test separately. It could be the case that only one part of the plant or bush is edible (like the fruit or leaves), while the rest are poisonous (such as the stem or roots). Each part of a specimen should be tested alone before consuming the whole plant.

2. Before trying it, do a skin contact test by rubbing the specimen on the inside of your forearm or your outer lips. Let that sit for 15 mins and if there is no sign of irritation, proceed with the next step.

3. Taste a small portion of it without swallowing and wait for 5 mins. If there is any sign of irritation or a strongly bitter/soapy flavor, spit it out immediately and rinse your mouth out with water.

4. If there is no irritation or overtly off-putting taste, take a teaspoon quantity of the specimen and chew for 5 mins. Spit out any extra saliva as you do this. Swallow, and give your body 8 hrs to react to the plant.

5. If no adverse reaction is experienced, consume a tablespoon worth of the plant and wait another 8 hours. If you still feel okay after this, and no digestive issues or weird symptoms arise, the plant is safe to eat, and the chances it might kill you are greatly reduced.

Before an edibility test, I'd advise you to study the fatally toxic plant species in your area. Many poisonous plants can cause mild illness and diarrhea, but a few others such as poison hemlock, which is fairly common, can easily result in death even if ingested in small amounts.

When it comes to foraging for food, it is important to seek out a location with a variety of habitats. Look for areas with open sunny spots, edges, fields, meadows, and woods to give yourself the best chance at finding a variety of edible plants. Different types of plants may favor different kinds of environments, and a diverse selection of habitats will give you the most options. Don't be afraid to venture out and explore different areas to see what types of edible plants you can find.

Now I will give some general guidelines when foraging for wild plants. I cannot give a comprehensive guide to foraging as every area has thousands of different plant, mushroom and insect species, and I highly recommend you pick up a local foraging guide.

I have to stress this again because it's so vitally important.

> **DO NOT EAT WILD PLANTS OR MUSHROOMS UNLESS IT IS A LAST RESORT AND YOU HAVE POSITIVELY IDENTIFIED WHAT IT IS.**

Now, here are several key things to look for to help identify safe plants to eat. Some general guidelines to follow include:

- ☐ Identify edible plants. The best thing you can do is to research which plants are edible in the area you are in, and make sure to double-check with a reliable source.
- ☐ Collect edible plants carefully. Avoid picking plants near

roads or industrial areas where they may be contaminated. Make sure to use gloves, and only pick plants that are in abundance.

☐ Wash plants before consumption. Make sure to clean off any dirt or debris off of the plant before consumption.

☐ Cook plants before consumption. Boiling or steaming plants will help to make them more digestible and reduce the chances of food poisoning. Some wild mushrooms and plants may contain toxins that can be eliminated or reduced by cooking.

☐ Look for plants that are common and widespread in your area. These are more likely to be safe to eat.

☐ Avoid plants that are rare or found only in a small area, as these may be more difficult to identify and may be poisonous.

☐ Avoid plants with spines, thorns, or hairs, as these can irritate your skin or mouth.

☐ Avoid plants with a bitter or soapy taste, as these may be toxic.

☐ Look for plants that have been eaten by animals, as these are more likely to be safe for humans to eat. However, some plants may be poisonous to humans even if they are safe for animals.

☐ Plants or berries with an almond-esque scent. Wild

plants with an almond-esque scent often contain cyanide compounds, which can be poisonous if consumed. It is best to avoid these plants and berries when foraging.

For mushrooms:

- ☐ Avoid mushrooms with brightly colored caps.
- ☐ Avoid mushrooms with a foul or unpleasant smell.
- ☐ Avoid mushrooms with a slimy or sticky texture.
- ☐ Avoid mushrooms with milky saps, fine hairs, and spines

Some edible mushrooms have brightly colored caps, unpleasant smells, and a slimy tecture, so not all mushrooms that meet these criteria are dangerous.

The same goes in reverse, not all plants that meet these criteria are necessarily safe to eat. Always do your research and make sure you are able to properly identify a plant before eating it.

Some of the most common mushrooms people forage for are:

- ☐ Giant puffballs (Calvatia gigantea) are large, round mushrooms with a white exterior and interior and a tough, leathery outer skin. They look like footballs and can grow up to a foot in diameter. They are commonly found in meadows, grassy fields, and wooded areas in the late summer and early fall. They can be found in Europe, North America, and some parts of Asia.

- ☐ Hedgehog mushrooms (Hydnum Repandum) have a yellow-orange, funnel-shaped cap and a spiny underside. They are commonly found in deciduous forests, growing in clusters at the base of trees. They can be found in Europe, North America, and some parts of Asia.

☐ Porcini are highly sought-after mushrooms that are prized for their nutty, earthy flavor. They have a white stem, a brown to yellow cap, and a spongy underside. They grow in moist, shady forests and can be found in parts of Europe, North America, and Asia.

☐ Chicken of the woods (Laetiporus sulphureus): Chicken of the woods are bright yellow-orange mushrooms with a soft, spongy texture. They're called chicken (or hen) of the woods because they are packed with protein, a vital thing to have in a survival situation. They grow on dead or dying hardwood trees and can be found in North America, Europe, and parts of Asia.

☐ Morels (Genus Morchella) are prized for their unique flavor and texture. They have a honeycomb-like, cone-shaped cap and a hollow stem. They are commonly found in deciduous forests in the spring and early summer. They can be found in Europe, North America, and some parts of Asia.

☐ Chanterelles (Genus Cantharellus) are trumpet-shaped mushrooms with a yellow to orange color. They have a fruity, apricot-like aroma and a nutty flavor. They are commonly found growing in clusters on the ground in deciduous and coniferous forests in the summer and fall. They can be found in Europe, North America, and some parts of Asia.

Guide To Medicinal Plants

If you live off-grid, or find yourself in an extended survival situation, it is important to have a plan for how to maintain your health. Part of this plan should include growing medicinal herbs. Medicinal herbs can be used to treat a wide variety of ailments, including pain, inflammation, and infections. They can also be used to boost immunity and energy levels. Having a supply of medicinal herbs on hand can help you stay healthy in a survival situation and improve your chances of making it through to safety.

Moringa

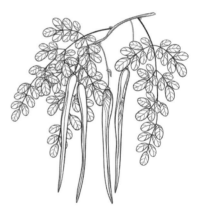

Moringa is a plant that is native to Africa and Asia. It is often referred to as the "miracle tree" due to its wide range of health benefits. Moringa can be used to treat a variety of ailments, including:

- Anemia: Moringa is a good source of iron, which can help to treat anemia.
- Asthma: Moringa can help to reduce inflammation and bronchial constriction, which can help to ease asthma symptoms.
- Diabetes: Moringa can help to regulate blood sugar levels, which can be beneficial for people with diabetes.

□ Digestive problems: Moringa can help to improve digestion and can also help to relieve constipation and diarrhea.

□ Heart health: Moringa can help to lower blood pressure and cholesterol levels, which can be beneficial for heart health.

□ Immune system: Moringa can help to boost the immune system.

How To Grow

1. To grow Moringa from seed, plant them directly in the ground where the tree is intended to grow.

2. Choose an area with light, sandy soil that is not heavy with clay or water-logged.

3. Dig holes 1 ft (30 cm) square and 1 ft deep, and backfill with loose soil.

4. If the soil is heavy, dig a larger hole of up to 3 ft (90 cm) in diameter and 3 ft deep, and backfill with 1 part sand and 2 parts original soil.

5. Add compost or manure to help the tree grow better.

6. Plant 3 to 5 seeds in each hole, 2 in. (5 cm) apart and no deeper than three times the width of the seed (approximately ½ in. or 1.5 cm -- the size of one's thumbnail).

7. Keep the soil moist but not too wet, as the seeds can drown and rot.

8. When the saplings are four to six inches tall, keep the healthiest sapling in the ground and remove the rest. Protect the saplings from termites and nematodes.

How To Harvest

1. Cut the branches of the moringa tree. Use pruning shears or a sharp knife to avoid damaging the tree. Choose branches that are at least eight inches long.

2. Remove the leaves from the branches. Gently pull the leaves off the branch in a downward motion.

3. Wash the leaves with cold water. Rinse the leaves off to remove any dirt or debris.

4. Dry the leaves in the sun. Spread the leaves out in a single layer on a baking sheet and place in direct sunlight for several hours.

5. Store the dried leaves in an airtight container. Place the leaves in a glass jar or other airtight container and store in a cool, dry place. The leaves can be used for up to a year.

How To Consume

- Make a tea: Boil 1 cup of water and add 1 teaspoon of dried moringa leaves. Simmer for 10 minutes, strain, and enjoy.

- Make a smoothie: Blend together 1 cup of milk, 1 banana, 1 tablespoon of ground up moringa leaves, 1 tablespoon of honey, and 1 teaspoon of cinnamon.

- Create a tincture: Soak 1/4 cup of moringa leaves in 1 cup of vodka for 10 days, strain, and store in a glass container. Take 1-2 teaspoons of the tincture per day.

- Cook with it: Add ground up moringa leaves to soups, stews, and curries for a nutritional boost.

Echinacea

Echinacea, also known as the coneflower, is an herb that is well known for its immune-boosting properties.

- Reducing inflammation: Echinacea is a natural anti-inflammatory agent, and can help to reduce swelling and redness in the body.

- Boosting the immune system: Echinacea is thought to stimulate the immune system, helping the body to better fight off infection.

- Fighting infections: Echinacea has natural antibacterial and antiviral properties, making it effective in fighting both bacterial and viral infections.

- Treating colds, flu, and other respiratory infections: Echinacea is often used as a natural treatment for colds, flu, and other respiratory infections. The herb is thought to help reduce symptoms and shorten the duration of these illnesses.

How To Grow

Echinacea is a hardy plant that can be grown in a variety of soil types and in full sun or partial shade. The plant is native to North America, and is commonly found in the eastern and central United States. Don't overwater! It prefers moist to dry soil.

How To Harvest

Echinacea can be harvested in the summer or fall, after the flowers have bloomed. The roots, leaves, and flowers of the plant are all edible, and can be used fresh or dried.

Garlic

Garlic is a common spice known for its pungent smell and health benefits. It is used in cooking to add flavor to food, but it is also used as a natural remedy for various ailments. Garlic is a member of the onion family and contains many of the same health-promoting compounds as onions, leeks, and chives. These compounds include sulfur-containing compounds, such as allicin, which have been shown to have antibacterial, antiviral, and antifungal properties. Garlic also contains antioxidants that can help protect cells from damage and reduce the risk of some chronic diseases, such as heart disease and cancer.

How To Grow

Garlic is a relatively easy plant to grow, and it can be done in either a garden bed or in containers.

To grow garlic in a garden bed, loosen the soil with a spade or tiller to a depth of 12 inches. Then, plant the cloves 4-6 inches apart and 1-2 inches deep, with the pointed end up. Water the bed well and keep it evenly moist throughout the growing season.

To grow garlic in containers, fill a pot that is at least 12 inches deep with a well-draining potting mix. Plant the cloves 4-6 inches apart and 1-2 inches deep, with the pointed end up. Water the container well and keep it evenly moist throughout the growing season.

How To Harvest

When the leaves start to yellow and die back, stop watering and allow the garlic to cure in the sun for 2-3 weeks. After curing, the garlic can be stored in a cool, dark place for up to 6 months.

How To Consume

Come on now, I shouldn't have to tell you how to eat garlic.

Ginger

Ginger is a popular home remedy for nausea, colds, and upset stomachs. It is also used to treat inflammation and pain. One of the most well-known benefits of ginger is its ability to settle the stomach. It can help relieve nausea and vomiting, and is often used as a natural treatment for morning sickness. Ginger is also a natural anti-inflammatory, which can help to reduce pain and swelling. Additionally, some research suggests that ginger may be effective in treating osteoarthritis, migraines and menstrual pain. It is also known for its immune-boosting properties.

How To Grow

Ginger is a tropical plant that is typically grown in warm, humid climates. It can be difficult to grow ginger in other climates, but it is possible to grow it indoors. To grow ginger, you will need to start with a piece of fresh ginger root. Plant the ginger root in a pot of well-drained soil, and water it regularly. The ginger root will sprout and eventually produce a small plant. Once the plant is established, you can harvest the ginger by digging up the root.

How To Consume

☐ Drink ginger tea: Boil 4-5 slices of fresh, grated ginger in two cups of water for 10 minutes. Strain the tea and drink it hot. Add honey or other natural sweetener for additional flavor.

☐ Make a ginger compress: Soak a cloth in a mixture of grated ginger and warm water. Apply the compress directly to the affected area

St. John's Wort

St. John's wort is an herbal supplement that has been traditionally used for centuries to treat a variety of conditions, including depression, anxiety, and sleep disorders. More recently, it has been shown to be effective in treating mild to moderate

depression. It is thought to work by increasing levels of serotonin, a neurotransmitter that is involved in regulating mood. It also looks beautiful, which should give you a mood boost on it's own.

How To Grow

St. John's wort can be grown from seed, but it is best to start with young plants because they are easier to care for and establish. Young plants also have a higher success rate than seeds. The seeds should be planted in well-drained soil in full sun to partial shade. The plants will need to be watered regularly, especially during the summer months. Once the plants are established, they will need little care other than occasional trimming to keep them from getting too large.

How To Harvest

St. John's wort can be harvested anytime during the growing season. Cut the stems just above where they branch off, and then strip the leaves from the stems. The leaves and flowers can be used fresh or dried for later use.

How To Consume

Brew St. John's Wort into a tea: To make a tea, steep 1 teaspoon of dried herb in 1 cup of boiling water for 10 minutes. Strain and sweeten with honey if desired. You can drink up to 3 cups daily.

Turmeric

Turmeric is a spice that is often used in Indian and Asian cuisine. It has a warm, earthy flavor and is frequently used to flavor or color curry powders, mustards, and other savory dishes.

Turmeric contains a compound called curcumin, which is responsible for its characteristic yellow color. Curcumin is a potent antioxidant and has anti-inflammatory properties. It has been used for centuries in traditional Indian and Chinese medicine to treat a variety of conditions, including digestive disorders, skin diseases, and wounds.

More recently, curcumin has been shown to have promise in the treatment of several chronic diseases, such as cancer, Alzheimer's disease, and diabetes. It may also help to improve cognitive function and to reduce inflammation in the brain.

How To Grow

- ☐ Turmeric is a tropical plant and cannot tolerate frost. It is best grown in a warm, humid climate.

- ☐ Turmeric can be grown from seed, but it is more commonly propagated from rhizomes (underground stems). Rhizomes should be planted in well-drained, loose soil in early spring.

- ☐ Turmeric plants need full sun and regular watering. They will spread rapidly and can become invasive if not kept in check.

How To Harvest

- ☐ Turmeric rhizomes are typically harvested after about 9-10 months. They can be used fresh or dried and ground into a powder.

- ☐ When using fresh turmeric, it is important to note that it can stain your hands and clothing. Wear gloves and old clothes when handling it.

- ☐ When using turmeric for medicinal purposes, it is important to start with a low dose and increase gradually as needed. High doses of turmeric can cause gastrointestinal upset.

How To Consume

- ☐ Turmeric Tea: Boil 2 cups of water and add 1 teaspoon of ground turmeric. Simmer for 10 minutes, then strain and add honey or lemon to taste.

- ☐ Turmeric Milk: Heat 1 cup of milk (dairy or non-dairy) and add 1 teaspoon of ground turmeric. Simmer for 5 minutes and strain before drinking.

- ☐ Turmeric Powder: Mix 1 teaspoon of ground turmeric with 1 teaspoon of honey and swallow.

Lavender

Lavender is a flowering plant that has been used for its medicinal properties for centuries. It has a soothing and calming effect, and has been used to help alleviate anxiety, stress, and insomnia. In addition to its calming effects, lavender has also been used to help with digestive issues, such as stomachache and bloating, and to help heal minor cuts and scrapes.

How To Grow

Choose a sunny spot with well-drained soil. Lavender prefers a slightly alkaline soil with a pH between 6.5 and 7.5. Plant your lavender in the spring, spacing the plants about 18 inches apart to allow for proper growth. Water your lavender regularly, but be careful not to over-water as this can lead to root rot.

How To Harvest

Cut the stems just as the flowers are starting to open. You can use scissors or garden shears for this. Be sure to cut the stems early in the morning, before the sun has had a chance to evaporate the oils from the flowers. This will help to preserve the essential oils that give lavender its medicinal properties.

How To Consume

To take lavender, you can make a tea by steeping a few sprigs of fresh lavender in hot water for several minutes. You can also use dried lavender in the same way. This is my personal favorite way to consume lavender.

Another option is to make a tincture by steeping fresh or dried lavender in alcohol for several weeks, then straining it to remove the plant material. You can then take the tincture by adding a few drops to water or juice.

Evening Primrose

The evening primrose (Oenothera biennis) is a flowering plant native to North America. It is a tall, upright plant with long, slender leaves and bright yellow flowers that bloom in the late afternoon and evening. The flowers have a sweet, pleasant aroma and are often used in herbal remedies for their medicinal properties.

The evening primrose plant has been used for centuries by Native American and European herbalists for a variety of ailments. The evening primrose plant has been used for its medicinal properties for centuries. The roots and leaves of the plant contain essential fatty acids, such as gamma-linolenic acid (GLA), which are believed to have anti-inflammatory and pain-relieving effects. The oil extracted from the seeds of the evening primrose plant is also rich in GLA, and is often used as a natural remedy for various skin conditions, such as eczema and acne.

In addition to its effects on the skin, the evening primrose plant has also been used to treat other conditions. Some studies have suggested that the GLA in the oil from the evening primrose seeds may be effective at reducing symptoms of premenstrual syndrome (PMS), such as bloating, breast tenderness, and mood swings. The plant has also been used to help alleviate menopausal symptoms, such as hot flashes and night sweats.

While the evening primrose plant has been used medicinally for centuries, more research is needed to fully understand its potential health benefits. It is important to consult with a healthcare provider before using the plant or its oil as a natural remedy, as it may interact with certain medications or underlying medical conditions.

In addition to its medicinal uses, the evening primrose is also a popular garden plant. It is easy to grow and thrives in well-drained soil with full sun exposure. The plant can reach heights of up to six feet, making it a striking addition to any garden. The bright yellow flowers of the evening primrose are also attractive to pollinators, such as bees and butterflies, making it a beneficial plant for supporting local ecosystems.

The evening primrose is a hardy, easy-to-grow plant that thrives in well-drained soil and full sun exposure.

How To Grow

1. Choose a sunny spot in your garden with well-drained soil. Evening primroses can tolerate a variety of soil types, but they prefer a slightly alkaline soil with a pH between 6.5 and 7.5.

2. Before planting, work some compost or well-rotted

manure into the soil to improve its drainage and nutrient content.

3. Sow the evening primrose seeds directly in the ground in early spring, as soon as the ground can be worked. Space the seeds about 12 inches apart, and cover them with a thin layer of soil.

4. Water the seeds well, and keep the soil moist until they germinate. This typically takes about 7-14 days.

5. Water the plants regularly, and apply a layer of mulch around the base of the plants to help retain moisture and suppress weeds.

6. Evening primroses are generally low-maintenance plants, but they may benefit from occasional fertilization. Use compost or a balanced, all-purpose fertilizer.

7. Enjoy the beautiful, fragrant flowers of the evening primrose as they bloom in the late afternoon and evening. The flowers are attractive to pollinators, such as bees and butterflies, making them a beneficial addition to any garden.

Flax

Flax is a plant that is known for its seeds, which are small, brown, and have a nutty flavor. The plant itself is a member of the Linaceae family, and it is native to the Mediterranean region. Flax is grown for its seeds, which are high in omega-3 fatty acids, fiber, and lignans.

The health benefits of flaxseed are believed to come from its high content of omega-3 fatty acids, which are essential fatty acids that the body cannot produce on its own. These fatty acids are thought to reduce inflammation in the body, which can help to prevent chronic diseases such as heart disease and cancer. Flaxseed is also a good source of fiber, which can help to lower cholesterol levels and improve digestive health.

In addition to its nutritional value, flaxseed is also used for its laxative effects, as the fiber in the seeds can help to promote regular bowel movements. Some people also use flaxseed oil as a natural remedy for a variety of skin conditions, such as eczema and psoriasis.

Overall, flax is a plant that has many potential health benefits, and can be a valuable source of calories in a survival situation.

How To Grow

To grow flax, you will need to start with flax seeds, which are available at many garden centers and online retailers.

1. Before planting, it's important to choose a location for your flax plants that has well-drained soil and full sun exposure. The seeds can be sown directly into the ground in the spring, after the last frost has passed.

2. To plant the seeds, first loosen the soil in the area where you will be planting the seeds, and then create shallow furrows in the soil with a hoe or rake.

3. Next, scatter the seeds evenly in the furrows, and then cover them with a thin layer of soil.

4. Water the area well, and keep the soil moist until the seeds have germinated, which typically takes about 7-10 days.

5. As the plants mature, they will produce small, blueish flowers, which will eventually be replaced by the seeds. When the seeds are ripe, they will turn brown and can be harvested.

To harvest the seeds, simply cut the stalks of the flax plants, and then allow them to dry for several days in a cool, dry place. Once the seeds are dry, you can thresh them by rubbing the stalks between your hands or by using a small tool like a flail. The seeds can then be collected and stored in an airtight container until you are ready to use them.

GARDENING PROJECTS

Gardening Projects

The most viable solution to long-term self-reliant survival is growing your own food. Learning how to grow your own food is an essential skill for anyone planning to be self-sufficient. If you know what it takes to grow and preserve your food, you are already in the top tier of preppers.

Preppers usually approach gardening with a different mindset. This is because modern farming relies on the assumption that gasoline, electricity, farming supplies, and water are readily available at all times. The style of gardening that's right for you depends on the type of crisis you are anticipating and your personal self-sufficiency goals. Another thing to consider is the location of your land. Learn about your hardiness zone, because that determines what grows well in your local climate. It's better to have experience in gardening, and a raised bed & compost setup built out, before you need it.

How To Build A Raised Garden Bed

Difficulty: Easy

Materials

- ☐ Two 8 ft x 1 ft x 1 in. boards
- ☐ Two 4 ft x 1ft x 1 in. boards (or cut an 8 ft board in half)
- ☐ 3-inch screws (at least 12)

Tools

- ☐ Power drill

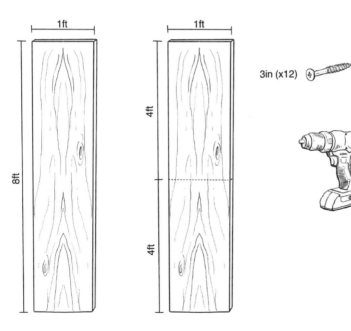

Steps

1. Pre-drill three screw holes at each end of the longer boards, space them out evenly so they can secure the short boards properly.

2. Pre-sink the screws halfway into the holes, so they do not fall off the boards.

3. Stand a long board against a short board so that they form a right angle at one end of the board, aligned with the screws. Make sure that the top and sides of both boards are flush against each other.

4. Drill in the top screw and check that both boards are properly aligned by pivoting the long board on the screw and realigning it with the short board if needed.

5. Drill in the bottom screw before you do the middle screw.

6. Repeat steps three to five for the other corners. At the end of the exercise, you will have a rectangular bed frame ready for planting.

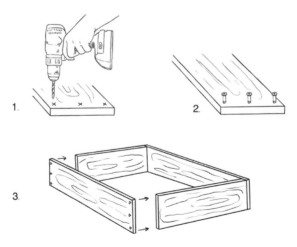

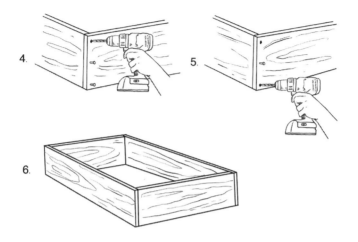

By deliberate design, this project gives you a low raised bed, but it is a good foundation for building a higher one. Instead of screwing the boards to each other, you will add corner posts to which you will attach the boards. The posts will provide stability to the structure as you build higher than one-foot aboveground.

If you do plan to create a high raised bed, say, hip-high, you can use fillers at the bottom of the bed, so it's not too expensive to fill with tons of soil. Some street-smart gardeners might put in large logs. Over the years, they will decompose and add themselves to the soil nutrients. If you had taken out your lawn grass to make space for your homestead garden, you can use the very same sod as filler by flipping it over, grass-side down. If you have pieces of old, untreated lumber, you can throw them in there, too. You can use any organic matter to throw into the high raised bed. Once you have taken care of the bottom part, you can devote your attention to the top layer.

How To Create Compost

Difficulty: Easy

The sooner you start composting the better. Not only is it great practice for when SHTF and you don't have access to commercial or inorganic fertilizer, but it is also free, and can be made from collecting the organic waste that comes out from your house (food scraps, dog poop, yard trimmings, etc). Composting takes time, the sooner you start building your pile the better.

There are a few different ways to compost. They are:

- □ Hot composting involves the decomposition of organic material by means of the heat they generate when you pile them up and leave them to the mercy of the elements. There are two types of hot composting:

- □ Aerobic composting requires you to turn the compost over every few days to introduce air inside the pile. It's a quick way to make your own fertilizer, but it does require a lot of energy from you for shoveling and raking. If done right, you can expect to use the compost in about 14 to 21 days.

- □ Anaerobic composting does not need your biceps for turning over. Just leave the scraps and stuff alone. They will decompose more slowly than with aerobic composting, usually taking four weeks to a year or more to do so.

- □ Vermicomposting is the decomposition of organic matter by employing worms and bacteria in moisture. The worms process the waste into nutrient-rich castings in a fast and efficient way.

How To Build A Vermicomposter

Difficulty: Easy

Materials

- ☐ Plastic container with lid (10+ gallon capacity)
- ☐ Sandpaper
- ☐ Newspapers
- ☐ 2 pounds of redworms,
- ☐ 1 pound of cut-up organic matter

Tools

- ☐ Drill and drill bits
- ☐ Kitchen scale
- ☐ Directions

Directions

1. Wash or wipe down the container and lid to get rid of residues that might kill the worms.

2. Use a small bit (1/8 inch) to drill some holes in the bottom of the container. Use a larger bit (at least ½ inch) to drill air holes on the top and around the sides near the brim. Sand down all sharp edges.

3. Prepare the worm bedding by doing the following:

4. Shred newspaper pages into tiny bits.

5. Soak them in water until spongy to the touch.

6.   Squeeze out excess water. The shredded paper should be moist, not dripping.

7.   Put the moist paper shreds into the worm bin. Do not pack them in; keep them loose and fluffed up. Fill the container to 3/4 capacity.

8.   Spread 2 lbs of worms evenly on top of the newspaper bedding and wait for them to burrow inside and out of sight.

9.   Once the worms are well hidden from view, place 1 pound of organic matter on the bedding, add another layer of bedding, and cover the container with its lid. If necessary, have a kitchen scale available to weigh both the worms and the organic matter.

And that's it! Caring for your vermicomposter is essential too.

Bin lid
Newspaper
Organic matter
Worms
Shredded newspaper

Here are some important things to keep in mind when raising these beautiful beasts.

- ☐ Make sure not to feed your worms more than half their body weight per week. Overfeeding can cause the vermicomposter to build up too much moisture and drown them. It can also cause unwanted rancid odors or make the worms sick.

- ☐ Keep the container in a safe, quiet, and dark place. The sweet spot would be a location that is constantly between 40 to 80 degrees Fahrenheit and far from regular household activity - many people keep their vermicomposter in the basement.

- ☐ Monitor the activity in your vermicomposter regularly. Make sure that the worms are active and the bedding is moist. Spray some water if it dries up. If too much moisture builds up on the inner wall of the container, either add dry newspaper shreds or reduce the amount of organic matter for feeding. That moisture is caused by a lack of fresh bedding or overfeeding.

Now for harvesting! When your worm castings have built up considerably inside the container, are black in color, and smell like earth after a downpour, they are ready to be harvested and used in your garden.

A Nice Cup Of Worm Tea

A common strategy is using your harvested worm castings to make worm tea. Personally, I don't do this, but I know many who swear by it. All you have to do is place your worm castings in a porous bag and steep it in a bucket of water overnight. You can also just throw the worm castings into the bucket in a pinch. Most of the nutrients are now in the water. Using the worm tea is simple: fill up a spray bottle and apply directly to your plants. You can also pour the worm tea directly into your garden if that sounds like too much work

How To Build A Hot Composter

Difficulty: Easy

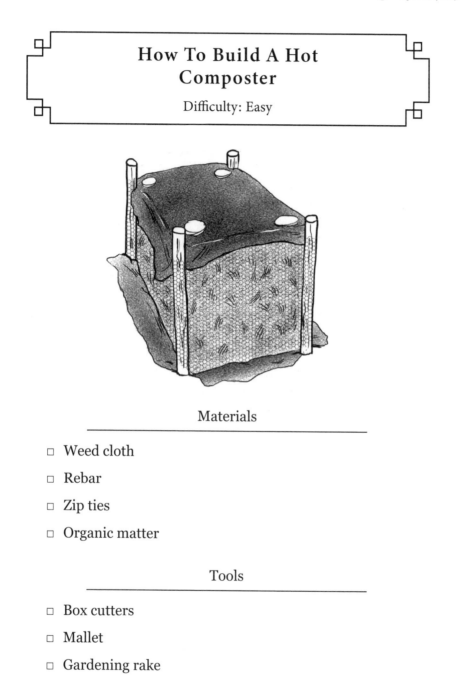

Materials

☐ Weed cloth

☐ Rebar

☐ Zip ties

☐ Organic matter

Tools

☐ Box cutters

☐ Mallet

☐ Gardening rake

Directions

1. Identify a place in your garden for the hot composter. Refer to your diagram from Step One in response to the question about space. I put mine a few feet beside an open shed, where I fixed things, transplanted seedlings, and stored materials. It was within reach of where I needed it the most.

2. Mark an area of 3 ft x 4 ft on the ground.

3. Measure the weed cloth to match the composting area and cut it to size.

4. Lay down the weed cloth on the ground and drive metal rebars through each corner to secure it.

5. Wrap durable netting material around the staked area and secure it to each rebar with zip ties. Ensure that the structure has no sharp points or edges protruding. Use the wire cutters to remove any.

6. Add organic matter by layers into the enclosed area, alternating it with a thin layer of soil and a sprinkle of water.

7. Cover the pile with weed cloth or netting material to keep the contents safe and secure from the wind and unwanted visitors, aka scavenging animals.

8. After three or four days, remove the cover and turn the pile over with a rake or shovel. Afterward, repeat steps 7 and 8 until all the organic matter is ready for harvesting. It is ready for use when it has the color of dark chocolate and smells and crumbles like moist loam. Replace the compost with fresh organic matter and begin again.

Regardless of which composting type you choose, only three ingredients are necessary to get started: browns, greens, and water. Water is self-explanatory. It is the medium for introducing essential bacteria into the mix. There has to be enough only to keep organic matter moist. It should not overwhelm the rest of the pile or drown the poor worms. Now, we just need to focus on browns and greens.

Browns are the organic materials that give you carbon, while greens provide nitrogen. I came up with a list for each type as your guide. It is a combination of information from the US Environmental Protection Agency and several other sources, including my own personal experience:

Browns	Greens
Branches (dead)	Banana peelings
Bread	Carrot tops
Cardboard (shredded)	Clover
Corncobs	Coffee filters (paper)
Cotton (no absorbed chemicals or substances)	Coffee grounds (soaked only in water)
Dryer lint	Feathers
Eggshells	Fruit scraps
Fireplace ashes (from firewood)	Grass clippings (hot composting only)
Flowers (dried)	Horse manure
Fur	Leaves (fresh)
Grains	Plants (fresh)
Hair	Potato skins
Hay	Seaweed
Leaves (dead)	Teabags
Newspapers (shredded)	Vegetable scraps
Nutshells	
Paper	
Paper towels (food-soiled)	
Pinecones	
Pine needles	
Plants (dead)	
Potting soil	
Sawdust	
Straw	
Twigs (dead)	
Vines (dead)	
Woodchips	
Wood shavings	
Wool rags (no absorbed chemicals or substances)	
Yard trimmings	

These are the things you should never throw into your composter and why, according to the EPA:

☐ Black walnut tree (any part): releases substances harmful to plants

- □ Coal or coal ash: may have substances toxic to plants
- □ Dairy products (milk, cheese, and the like): invite rats and flies and stink
- □ Disease- or pest-infested plants: may transfer infestations to other plants
- □ Fat, grease, lard, and oils: produce odors and attract pests
- □ Meat or fish bones and scraps: create foul smells, and invite pests and strays
- □ Pet wastes: may contain harmful bacteria, parasites, pathogens, and viruses
- □ Yard trimmings (chemical-treated): may kill beneficial composting organisms

How To Build A Hugelkultur Mound

Difficulty: Medium

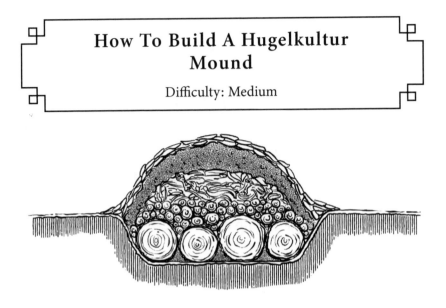

Hugelkultur is the practice of planting on top of lots of buried organic material. This is done by burying different types of organic material of different sizes in a mound. Once constructed, your hugelbed will provide highly enriching soil for your plants for years to come. The best part? Because of the way it's built, it will require minimal watering, tilling, or maintenance. Hugelkultur is perfect during a grid down disaster because you may not have access to running water, fertilizers or other additives you typically add to your soil.

So what exactly is inside a hugelbed? There are generally 5 layers:

1. The innermost stratum of a hügelbed is made up of logs. They will compost slowly to become humus, a plant superfood. Logs also absorb water efficiently, making them something of a godsend in places that lack an abundance of rainfall. The wood at the core of the mound is supposed to be of significant size and/or quantity to soak up as much water/moisture as possible. Smaller

branches are piled right over the medium/big wood pieces to add to the mass.

2. After the wood layer comes the layer made up of compostables. They could be made of upside-down turf, wood chips, grass clippings, manure, leaves, sticks, twigs, vegetable peels, etc. It can be a single layer or multiple layers of varying/ alternating materials. The key is to fill in the gaps among the branches and logs to make a compact, solid hillock that won't cave in at the first rainfall or your golden retriever's paws.

3. The third layer is compost, whether from a compost heap or a vermicomposter. It's different from the second layer in that it's already been processed by time and the natural elements.

4. The fourth layer is your garden soil, fine compost, or any growing medium/mix, which acts as the topsoil.

5. The fifth and final tier is mulch to protect the hügelbed from erosion.

The different layers and materials work together to give your hugelbed it's magic. The compost provides immediate nutrients to your soil, while the compostables give it a boost in the months to come. The logs are excellent at water retention, and create an environment that requires minimal watering (after the initial setup). Over the years, the logs also break down, giving your plants a slow drip of nutrients.

Materials

- ☐ Logs (3 to 12 inches in diameter)
- ☐ Tree branches

☐ Twigs

☐ Leaves

☐ Grass clippings

☐ Vegetable and fruit remains

☐ Flattened old cardboard boxes

Tools

☐ Shovel

☐ Hoe

☐ Ax or saw

☐ Measuring tape

Directions

1. Measure a space of 6 feet by 5 feet on the ground and mark it.

2. Carefully remove any grass or turf intact on top of the marked area and set it aside.

3. Dig a 6-inch-deep trench within the rectangle. Even out the bottom to ensure a flat surface on which to build layers.

4. [Optional] Cover the bottom completely with flattened cardboard boxes to act as a weed-and-pest barrier.

5. Arrange large pieces of deadwood lengthwise (6 feet) in the middle of the trench. If needed, cut them down to size with an ax or a saw. Don't spread the wood pieces beyond 2 feet wide. Water generously.

6. Place smaller pieces of deadwood on top of the large

ones. Cut them smaller, if necessary. The total height of the woodpile should be no more than 15 inches. Water generously .

7. Pack in leaves, grass clippings, and other similar greens. Make sure to push them into the small spaces among the wood pieces. Keep the entire construction compact. This layer should be no more than 12 in deep. Water generously .

8. If you have turf, place it on top of the woodpile, with the green side facing down. Cover the entire first layer.

9. If you have a compost pile or a vermicomposter, add a compost layer of no more than 6 in. This is now your brown layer. If you don't have one, add vegetable and fruit cuttings mixed with soil. Follow the same recommended depth for the compost layer. Water generously.

10. On top of the coarse compost layer, add topsoil, ideally loamy and fine-grained. This layer is also 6 in deep. Set the final layer in place by firmly tapping it in with the backside of a shovel or hoe. Water generously.

If you follow this basic construction guide, you'll end up with a mound around three feet high. It will have a base 6 feet long and 5 feet wide. Once it's finished, you may leave it idle for a few days. Give the materials some time to settle. Some people like planting on it immediately to ride the momentum and excitement of its construction. My best advice is to give it some time. Depending on your hügelbed content and final form, there's a possibility of the whole thing shifting a bit until it becomes compact and immoveable.

a.

b.

c.

d.

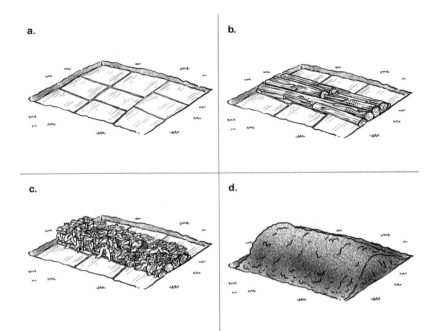

TRAPPING PROJECTS

Trapping Projects

Everyone and their mom will be out hunting when things get desperate. Being in a wilderness potentially full of inexperienced/trigger-happy people is risky. Still, if you know how to hunt efficiently, that risk is reduced, and the nutritional returns could be massive.

A much more realistic survival skill to learn is trapping. After all, your hands might be full, protecting your supplies and your family. Hunting requires a lot of time and patience, and being away from your main resources for too long is not ideal. Trapping is more efficient because you can set up multiple traps and focus on other things, like procuring water, foraging, building a shelter, or tending the garden. Trapping allows you to multitask and carries much less risk than hunting, exposing you to danger for prolonged periods with no guarantee of success.

The effort involved is much less intensive than hunting. Strategically placed traps and some bait is all you need for your food to come to you. The best places to set traps include:

- ☐ Along trails
- ☐ Around animal droppings and tracks
- ☐ Den holes and nesting sites
- ☐ Feeding sites (chewed vegetation) and watering holes

How To Build A Snare

Difficulty: Easy

Snares are mostly made to catch small game, especially rabbits and squirrels. Essentially, you are creating a noose that tightens under the weight of a hopping animal, so all you need is a wire.

1. Obtain bendable wire roughly 2.5 feet in length.

2. At the end of the wire, make a slip-knot loop, twisting the excess around the wire six times. Use pliers to clamp the twisted part of your knot.

3. Push the other end of the wire through the loop to create the noose, and pull until the new loop is roughly the size of a rabbit's head, roughly 7 inches.

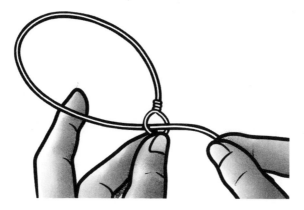

4. Tie the end to a stake. You may have to drill a hole in the stake. Firmly drive the stake into the ground of an area that rabbits frequent. If the stake is not posted firmly, then the rabbit will escape. Give the stake a tug to double-check how secure it is.

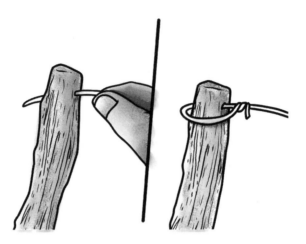

5. Use a stick to prop up the other end of the noose.

6. When the animal hops or runs through the hoop, the noose will tighten and either hold or kill it.

7. Check your traps at 24-hour intervals. You don't want to leave your catch for another predator.

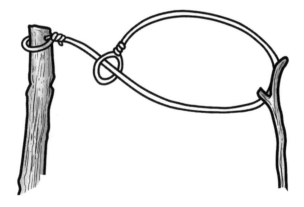

Hanging snare

A hanging snare works using the same principle. The noose will hang vertically from a bar, which should be secured and sturdy enough to hold a rabbit. The noose should be hanging roughly 7-8 inches above the ground. Place large branches on the sides and underneath the bar to increase the odds of a rabbit jumping through.

For the best results, place your traps near small/beaten paths, openings on fences, and in tall grass. Trapping is a numbers game; set as many as you can and wait patiently.

Squirrel snare

These were once used extensively during the time of the founding fathers. Squirrels are lazy; when you prop a branch or log against a tree, they always take the easiest route when climbing down. Lining up that log with snares is highly efficient. Squirrels are also curious and will go down the log to investigate why a fellow squirrel is hanging dead. Squirrels may not be your first choice for a meal, but many pioneers survived on them.

Mousetraps

Eating something off a mouse trap might be revolting, but they can capture any small critter roaming the wilderness. Also, the taste of mice/rats will be very palatable if starvation is the only alternative. A quality mousetrap can even catch a small rabbit, they are useful to have around, and everyone knows how to set them up.

How To Build A Tripwire Alarm

Difficulty: Easy

If SHTF, there could be a breakdown of law and order. Protecting yourself from any trespassers potentially bearing a nefarious agenda becomes essential. Knowing how to set up a tripwire alarm around the perimeter of your property could alert you to the presence of an intruder, allowing you to act promptly and prepare yourself for a potential confrontation (or cause an intruder to flee).

This project can also be useful for those who enjoy camping and want extra peace of mind when out in bear territory.

Materials

- ☐ Nylon thread (Preferably black)
- ☐ Piezo buzzer alarm (Any model that works between 6-14 volts)
- ☐ A 9-volt battery
- ☐ A 9-volt battery snap
- ☐ A large clothespin
- ☐ Any small thin piece of plastic, like a playing card
- ☐ Glue
- ☐ 2 Half-inch brass/stainless steel bolts
- ☐ 2 Thin nails
- ☐ Electrician tape

Tools

- ☐ Drill

- ☐ Flat file (optional)

- ☐ Hammer

Directions

1. Drill a small hole in the clothespin; it should be right above where the clothespin contacts are clamped shut. Use a drill bit that is the same diameter as the half-inch-long round-head bolts. Start drilling from the top and penetrate to the bottom. Be sure not to drill too wide of a hole at once; it will crack the wood. If the wood cracks, tightly wrap the clothespin with tape and drill the hole again.

2. Add some glue beneath the head of the brass round head bolts and insert them through the holes we made in step 1. The idea is to make the heads (of the brass bolts) come in contact with each other when the clothespin is shut.

3. Remember that the buzzer alarm will later be glued to the clothespin next to the brass bolt. Take note of the

two wires coming from the alarm, and cut the red wire to an appropriate length. Strip the end of the wire, loop it around the bolt shank, and then cover up the connection with electrician tape.

4. Glue the buzzer alarm to the clothespin. At this point, the red wire is connected to the brass bolt, and the black wire is still free.

5. Glue the 9-volt battery to the clothespin right beside the alarm.

6. Make a small hole through the piece of thin plastic and tie the nylon thread through it. Place the thin plastic sheet between the contacts before proceeding with the next step; otherwise, the alarm will go off.

7. Secure the 9-volt snap to the battery, and cut its black wire to a short length. Enough to connect/solder with the alarm's black wire we left hanging earlier. Connect the red wire to the opposing brass head using the electrical tape (same as step 8). Make sure all wires are trimmed accordingly. A wiring diagram is shown below.

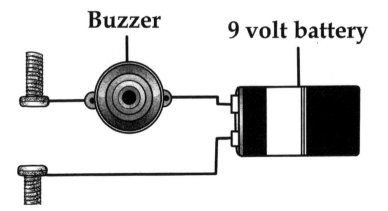

8. Test your system by pulling on the thread tied to the

small sheet of plastic. If the alarm goes off after the plastic barrier gets yanked away, you have successfully made a DIY trip alarm. All that's left is to find the perfect place to set it up.

9. If the alarm does not sound, try filing the brass heads, so they have more contact surface area or changing out components.

10. Secure the alarm to a tree or stake by putting a nail through the spring. Add another nail underneath the alarm so it can rest and doesn't pull out the card itself by spinning.

11. Keep in mind that these electrical components aren't meant to be outside in the elements. If you want to weatherproof this trap, I recommend putting this circuit in a waterproof case like a capped PVC pipe.

This project can be modified by adding more powerful speakers or batteries. The battery can be removed from the clip if it gets too heavy. Remember, more voltage generally makes the speaker louder.

CHICKEN PROJECTS

Chicken Projects

One of the best ways to maintain a high-protein food source when you can't go to the grocery store, is to raise chickens. They are relatively easy to care for and don't require a lot of space. Hens can turn bugs and scraps into protein and vitamin rich eggs every single day. They can also help with pest control. I have a whole book on raising chickens, called Raising Chickens for the First Time. Check it out if you're interested in learning more.

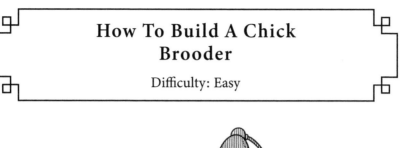

How To Build A Chick Brooder

Difficulty: Easy

Materials

- ☐ Large, recycled cardboard boxes

- ☐ Tape

- ☐ 3 pounds rough sand

- ☐ Old newspaper

- ☐ Two desk lamps with incandescent bulbs

- ☐ Small bowls/containers that can hold feed and water
  Hardware cloth (to cover the top of the cardboard box)

Tools

- ☐ Wire cutters
- ☐ Box cutters

Steps

1. Flatten the cardboard boxes and cut them at one edge, opening them up into a sheet.

2. Tape the cardboard sheets together at each edge (not the side with the flaps), so you get a continuous sheet.

3. Place the cardboard sheet on the ground of your designated brooder area with the flaps folded inside so the sheet stands up on its own.

4. Quickly calculate if the space enclosed is enough. Remember, you want one square foot of space for each chick. If you don't have enough space, add more box panels into your construction. If you do have enough space, great, tape the unconnected edge, and you should have an enclosure.

5. Line the bottom of the box with newspaper.

6. Cover the newspaper-lined bottom with rough sand to a depth of at least a couple of inches.

7. Place the food and water containers to one side of the box, leaving the rest of the space for the chicks to run around in.

8. Position the desk lamp (or two, depending on the size of the box) to the side opposite of the chicks' food and water, so they can eat and drink away from the heat it generates.

Check that it does have incandescent bulbs, which generate heat. Any other type of bulb will not produce the kind of heat necessary for the brooder to work properly.

9. Set the level of the desk lamp 18 to 20 inches above the chicks if you're in a cold area. Place it at 24 to 27 inches if your area is warmer. You may adjust up or down further, depending on the reaction of the chicks. If it's at a comfortable heat level, they will stay under it and act normally, pecking on the ground and walking about. They're not supposed to avoid it or run away from it. The recommended bulb for the desk lamp is incandescent and no more than 40 watts.

10. Flatten the hardware cloth and cut it with the wire cutters to a size that covers the top of the box. Cover the top of the box to prevent the chicks from hopping out of the brooder. Ensure that the hardware cloth doesn't have holes large enough for the chicks to jump through. If they regularly jump and push the cloth off, look into taping a hinge on one side and putting a fastener on the other.

With that, the brooder is ready to receive its temporary residents.

How To Farm Black Soldier Flies

Difficulty: Easy

Chicken feed is relatively inexpensive (although prices seem to keep going up), however, you can't always rely on Tractor Supply being open. Your chickens can forage for bugs and scraps, but if there isn't enough land for them to find food, you will need to supplement their diet. How does free, nutrient-rich, self-harvesting food for your chickens sound? Let me introduce you to the Hermetia Illucens, the Black Soldier Fly.

Black soldier fly larvae (BSFL) farming can bring down the expenses for feed to nearly zero. Like composting, these larvae eat organic waste material and upcycle it into a high-quality protein feed that is great for your chickens and their eggs. BSFL can also be fed to pigs, fish, and if times are really tough, to humans (they are calorie-rich and safe to eat).

BSFL are rich in the right amino acids your birds need. They also don't carry or transmit diseases, unlike houseflies. Recent studies at North Carolina State University have shown that BSFL can be a great addition to chicken feed for both egg-laying and broiler chickens. You'd be surprised at how easy it is to set up. A small BSFL build will upcycle your food scraps into a quality, protein-rich food your chickens will love. BSFL will eat pretty much anything you give them, increasing in size from a tiny 1mm to 25mm in just 2-3 weeks! Once the larvae have reached the adult stage and are ready to cocoon and turn into flies, they will crawl up the ramps you put for them and harvest themselves for you. It literally couldn't get any easier!

Materials

- ☐ 20 gallon plastic bin (or bigger) 5 gallon collection bucket
- ☐ 10 ft of 2" PVC pipe
- ☐ 90 degree PVC elbow joints (2x)

Tools

- ☐ Drill
- ☐ Saw

Steps

1. (Optional) Place two levels of cinder blocks flat on the ground. They will keep your setup off the ground and out of reach of pesky rodents. It will also allow for better air circulation.

2. (Optional) Place your plastic bin on top of the cinder blocks. Drill several drainage holes into the bottom of the bin to prevent liquid buildup. Cover the holes with hardware cloth to prevent the larvae from crawling out.

3. Cut your PVC pipe into two long and two short segments. Saw the long segments as shown in the image.

4. Cut two 2" holes near the top of one side of the bin. Put the PVC pipes through them. Make the slope as shallow as possible to aid the larvae when they're ready to crawl out. Less than 35 degrees is preferable.

5. Connect the angle joints and the small pipes to lead into the collection bucket.

6. Fill the bottom of the bin with old (used) bedding from your coop, brooder, or incubator. You can use newspapers, wood chips, compost, or dirt if you don't have any.

7. Layer the old bedding with rice bran until it's fully covered. Wet the bran to attract female black soldier flies. Moistened bran exudes a scent that attracts female BSF to the farm. Instead of bran, you can also use ground corn, fruit and vegetable scraps, or horse feed. They particularly like decaying food.

8. Hang corrugated cardboard from the sides or the lid of the bin. You can also place it on top of the bedding and bran. And then put the lid back on.

9. Create small holes around the top of the sides of the bin to allow adult flies to come in and lay their eggs.

10. Place the set up somewhere with a mix of shade and sun,

so it doesn't get too hot.

You can pretty much add any sort of food scraps or organic matter to the BSFL harvester. Meat, dairy, vegetable scraps, grains, composting, or decaying material. Monitor the bin daily. Top up the food supply if you see it running low. If the farm is working correctly, the BSFL should be running through the food you give them.

Attracting the Flies

The Black soldier fly originated in the Americas but is now present across most temperate regions in the world. Once the temperature is in the 70's Fahrenheit, adult black soldier flies will start laying eggs. That's when you want to load the harvester up with scraps to attract the adult females, so they lay their eggs in the bin. They deposit their "babies" near their food. The corrugated cardboard is an ideal surface for them to lay their eggs. At first, you might see other flies in the bin, but in a couple of weeks, you should see the black soldier fly larvae take over. It'll take a while, but you'll eventually get the flies you and your chickens want. If you can't attract them, you can also buy some live BSFL online and use that to start your colony. Once there is an active population, they will produce a mild odor that will attract female adults to lay their eggs there, furthering the cycle.

Female black soldier flies can lay as many as 500 eggs at a go, usually in surface gaps, hence, the corrugated cardboard. The eggs will take around four days to hatch into larvae. From that stage, give them two weeks to grow to about an inch before they start self-harvesting. When they're grown, they will crawl right up the PVC ramps and drop into your bucket, ready for you to feed to your chickens. Once in the bucket, they will cocoon and turn into flies in about a week, so I'd recommend checking the bucket and emptying it out every couple of days. If there are too many BSFL to feed to the chickens, dry them or freeze them for use in the winter months. They won't be active in the winter, but you'll have free chicken feed when the weather warms back up come springtime. With your own supply of nutritious chicken feed, you can reduce feed costs and just be that little bit more self- sufficient.

SHELTER PROJECTS

Shelter Projects

In a wilderness survival situation, it is important to have a shelter that provides additional protection beyond the clothing you are wearing. Retaining body heat is crucial when exposed to the elements. The location of your temporary shelter is also important and should be chosen carefully. The following factors should be considered when selecting a site for your shelter: the availability of natural resources such as water and firewood, the presence of natural shelter such as trees or cliffs, and the potential for hazards such as flooding or wildlife.

How To Keep Warm Without Power

Difficulty: Easy

Winter is arguably the worst time to experience a grid-down situation. However, keeping yourself and loved ones warm without gas or electricity is much more manageable when you're inside the house. Here are some tips to keep hypothermia at bay.

1. Clothes, and lots of them. Layer up and make sure there are enough barriers between your skin and the cold outside world. This is your first and most effective line of defense, fleece lined pants or tights are excellent to have. Wrap yourself with blankets for extra measure.

2. Keep the heat your body emits contained in a small space and spend the majority of your time there. Setting up a tent in a self-contained room is a good choice. If you don't have a tent, then make a fort by spreading your blankets over a table for a tent-like effect.

3. If you have them, keep hand and feet warmers in your gloves and socks

4. Make use of afireplace if you have one, use it to heat stones or bricks which you can remove with tongs and wrap in blankets to keep beds, sleeping bags or bodies warm. If you aren't using your fireplace, then tightly close off the damper to prevent hot air from escaping out through the chimney.

5. Buy an indoor portable stove for cooking, hot food keeps you warm and boosts morale. Be careful about carbon

monoxide buildup.

6. Cover windows with blankets or bubble wrap for insulation

7. Cover the undersides of your doors to block any drafts from entering.

8. Sleep with your family and cuddle up well. Bring in pets for extra warmth.

9. Move your body and get a little bit of exercise to increase body heat.

10. Keep babies and toddlers close and carry them with a sling to share your warmth.

11. Any hardwood, vinyl, concrete, or ceramic floors should be covered with rugs or blankets. A significant amount of heat is lost through floors alone.

12. Always wear shoes and socks

13. Heat rises. Stay on the upper floors if possible.

How To Keep Cool Without Power

Difficulty: Easy

Hyperthermia and heat stroke are real. With the US, UK, and many other parts of Europe experiencing record-setting heat waves, I sense the importance of keeping cool will greatly increase, especially in the absence of electricity. Below are some measures you can take to cool the house during the summer when the grid goes down.

1. Again, heat rises, so if you have a basement, that would be the coolest place. Basements are partially underground and are typically 10-15 degrees cooler than the rest of the house.

2. If you have solar energy, a dehumidifier can cool your house with relatively low energy costs (compared to an air conditioner). When it is both hot and humid, sweat can't evaporate, making it harder for the body to cool down. Dehumidifiers also collect water from the air, which is a bonus.

3. Grow vines outside your walls, but be careful not to damage them, and do your research to ensure your wall is compatible with the vine you want to plant. When done right, vines can significantly lower the home's temperature.

4. Plant trees around your home, they can also significantly reduce the temperature of the air around them. While waiting for your trees to grow, you can build shading structures like outdoor shutters or awnings for immediate

shade.

5. If it gets unbearable, dampen curtains or place wet blankets over the windows.

6. Prepare and cook food outdoors. Cooking generates a lot of heat that will linger.

7. Use fans to circulate air and create a cooling breeze. Ceiling fans can be particularly effective as they cool the entire room.

8. Use reflective window coverings, such as blinds or shades, to reflect sunlight and prevent it from heating up the house.

9. Consider installing a green roof or a white roof, which can help to reflect sunlight and reduce the amount of heat absorbed by the house.

10. Use your appliances wisely. Avoid using the oven or other heat-generating appliances during the hottest part of the day, and try to do laundry and other tasks that generate heat in the early morning or evening when it is cooler.

Considerations For Building A Survival Shelter

Location

When choosing a location for your shelter in a wilderness survival situation, it is important to find a spot that is high, dry, and sheltered from the elements. Avoid low-lying areas that are prone to flooding, and try to find a spot with natural windbreaks such as trees or cliffs. If there are cold winds, finding a spot with trees can provide additional protection, but be aware that breezes can also help keep bugs away.

In a rescue situation, being in a high location can make it easier for rescuers to spot you. However, if being seen could compromise your safety, you will need to choose a location that is as unobtrusive and hidden as possible. Camouflaging your shelter with leaves and branches can help to keep it from being noticed by potential threats.

Avoid setting up your shelter near game trails, as wild predators and unknown hunters may be lurking in the area. If you are planning to build a long-term shelter, make sure the ground is flat and stable, and check for signs of flooding before starting construction. Building a long-term shelter on a flood-prone site is a waste of time and energy, so it is important to choose a location carefully.

Duration of stay

Building a long-term shelter is not always a feasible option in
a survival situation. In most cases, it will only be necessary if
your home is no longer accessible or if returning to civilization is
impossible or unsafe. This could happen if you are stranded on
an island, lost in a forest, or fleeing from a deadly pandemic. In
these situations, building a long-term shelter may be necessary to
protect yourself from the elements and other hazards.

However, it is important to remember that in a truly catastrophic
event, society as we know it may collapse, and traditional ways
of living may no longer be feasible. In these situations, it may be
more practical to adopt a nomadic lifestyle, moving periodically to
find food and water rather than trying to grow your own food and
build a permanent structure. In the short term, your focus should
be on acquiring the skills and resources necessary to find food and
water, rather than building a long-term shelter.

In an off-grid survival situation, your ability to make a fire will be
critical for cooking food, boiling water, and providing warmth.
This skill should be a priority, as it will be more useful in the short
term than the ability to build a long-term structure.

Avoid sleeping directly on the ground

Sleeping directly on the ground can expose you to moisture,
insects, and other hazards. Elevating your sleeping mat, whether
on a bed frame, a platform, or a hammock, can help to keep you
dry and comfortable. In the winter, sleeping on snow or moist soil
can lead to hypothermia, so it is important to avoid direct contact
with the ground if possible.

If you don't have a tent or other shelter, a tarp or blanket can be repurposed into a makeshift hammock to elevate you off the ground. Alternatively, you can try building a cocoon-like structure using natural materials such as leaves and branches. This can provide some insulation and protection from the elements, but it will not be as effective as a dedicated shelter.

How To Build A Makeshift Shelter

Difficulty: Easy

If you find yourself in a survival situation without access to a tent, tarp, or hammock, you will need to make do with what nature has to offer. In general, the larger an emergency shelter, the more difficult it is to keep warm. Therefore, when building a temporary makeshift shelter, the ideal size will depend on the number of people who need to be accommodated. For a single person, the shelter should be large enough to fit their body. For a group, the shelter should be just large enough for everyone to huddle together for warmth.

In a crisis situation, it is important to prioritize warmth and protection from the elements. A makeshift shelter may not be as comfortable or spacious as a dedicated outdoor shelter, but it can provide vital protection from the weather and other hazards. By choosing the right location, materials, and design, you can build a makeshift shelter that is adequate for your needs.

Cocoon

A cocoon shelter is the most basic form of shelter that can be built in a survival situation, using only natural materials that are readily available in the environment. To build a cocoon shelter, you will need to gather a large quantity of leaves, bark, pine needles, or other dry materials from the forest floor. These materials should be piled up to a height of 2-3 feet, forming a mound that is large enough to accommodate your body.

Once the mound is built, you can burrow into it, using your body to create a hollow space inside the cocoon. This will help to insulate you from the cold ground, and it will retain some of your body heat to keep you warm. It is important to cover as much of your exposed skin as possible with clothing, as this will help to protect you from insects and other critters that may be attracted to the warmth of the cocoon.

A cocoon shelter is not a long-term solution, and it is not as effective as a dedicated shelter or tent. However, in a crisis situation, it can provide some basic protection from the elements and keep you warm until you can build a more permanent structure or find other shelter. A cocoon shelter is a last resort when you have no other options available.

Basic Lean-to

A lean-to shelter is a simple structure that can be built in a survival situation using natural materials found in the environment. To build a lean-to shelter, you will need to find a sturdy rock, fallen tree, or small overhang to serve as the wall of your shelter. Next, gather fallen branches and lean them against the wall, creating a sloping roof for your shelter.

To reinforce the shelter and protect against the elements, you can pile additional branches, leaves, bark, and other materials on top of the roof and against the open side of the shelter. This will create a less sturdy but effective wall that can help to shield you from rain and wind.

A fire on the open side of the lean-to can provide additional heat and light, and it can help to keep you warm and comfortable during the night.

How To Build An A-Frame Shelter

Difficulty: Easy

An A-frame shelter is a simple and effective structure that can provide basic shelter and protection in the wild. By using only natural materials and some basic construction techniques, you can build an A-frame shelter that will help you to stay warm and dry in a survival situation.

To build an A-frame shelter in the wild, you will need the following materials:

- ☐ Two sticks that are approximately 4 feet long
- ☐ One longer stick that is about 10 feet long
- ☐ A shoelace or belt

Follow these steps to build your A-frame shelter:

1. Find a suitable location for your shelter, away from water sources and potential hazards like landslides or falling trees.

2. Prop the two shorter sticks against each other in a capital 'A' shape, with the longer stick at the top, sloping down until it reaches the ground.

3. Tie the three sticks together at the top using the shoelace or belt, ensuring that the 'A' shape is sturdy and stable.

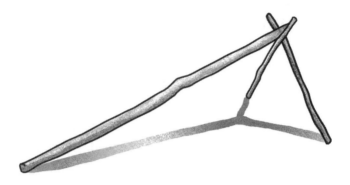

4. Lean additional sticks and dry debris against the long stick on both sides of the 'A' shape, creating a small, tapered shelter that slopes down to the ground.

5. Use leaves, bark, or other natural materials to insulate the shelter and protect it from the elements.

6. Once your shelter is built, test it for stability and comfort before settling in for the night.

7. If possible, build a fire on the open side of the shelter to provide additional warmth and light.

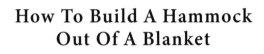

How To Build A Hammock Out Of A Blanket

Difficulty: Easy

Building a blanket hammock is a useful skill to have in a survival situation, as it can provide a comfortable and adequate shelter using only a blanket and some basic materials. This method is particularly useful if you have a wool blanket, as wool is able to retain heat even when wet.

To build a blanket hammock, you will need the following materials:

- ☐ A blanket, preferably queen-sized
- ☐ Four sturdy sticks, each about 15-20 inches long
- ☐ Mule tape, about 100 feet (you will not need to use all of it)

*Side point: Mule tape is a very handy item to have in a survival situation due to its light weight and high tensile strength. Many types of shelters can be made with mule tape.

Procedure

1. Spread a blanket on the ground in a diamond fashion and place one stick roughly a foot from one of the corners.

2. Envelop the stick by rolling the flap over it, making a triangle.

3. Place the second stick on top of the flap beside the first stick. A layer of the blanket should separate the two sticks.

4. Wrap the two sticks tightly with the blanket by rolling them a couple of times inwards.

5. Run the mule tape, starting from the middle of the two sticks, and tie them up in a figure 8 knot. Wrap the rope around the first stick once, then change direction to wrap the second stick, and repeat. In this figure 8 style, loop

your mule tape around the sticks 3-4 times.

6.   Run your mule tape around your selected tree, and repeat for the other end of the stick

7.   To secure it, finish off with a basic half-hitch knot. To do this, grab the end of the rope and turn it inwards to create a small noose, and place it through the middle of the sticks, in the opposite direction to the way you have been tying the figure-8 knot. The half-hitch knot is a simple and effective way to secure the dowel to the trees and prevent it from unraveling. It is important to tie the knot in the correct direction so that it tightens when the hammock is in use.

8.   Repeat the same process with the opposite corner of the blanket. When you apply weight to the blanket, the sticks

will try to unroll, but they can't because of the tension caused by the figure 8 style wrap and the knot.

This method does not require cutting the mule tape; you will have plenty left over for other uses. If you have 100 feet of it to work with, you will have plenty left over, which can be used to tie a ridgeline over the hammock and use a second blanket as an emergency tarp if needed. The blanket hammock is easy to set up and take down, providing a comfortable and sheltered sleeping area in most weather conditions. You don't need to cut your mule tape.

This method is one of the easiest ways to make a hammock from any type of blanket or suitable material and will keep you off the ground for a much greater quality of sleep. Roughing it on the ground is not ideal for a number of reasons.

How To Create A Makeshift Tent

Difficulty: Easy

If you have a tarp or blanket, you can also use it for a makeshift emergency tent, where you tie the mule tape a few feet above the ground between two trees to create a ridgeline.

Materials

- [ ] Two trees that are approximately the same size and distance apart

- [ ] Mule tape or another strong, durable rope

- [ ] A blanket, preferably made of wool or another insulating material

- [ ] Several medium-sized stones or rocks

Directions

1. Find a suitable location for your tent, away from water sources and potential hazards like landslides or falling trees.

2. Tie one end of the mule tape to one of the trees, ensuring that it is securely attached.

3. Tie the other end of the mule tape to the second tree, creating a taut line between the two trees.

4. Drape the blanket or tarp over the mule tape, allowing it to droop down to the ground on either side.

5. Spread the blanket apart and place the stones along the edges to hold it in place, creating an opening for a person to lay underneath.

With these steps, you can create a makeshift tent using mule tape, a blanket, and some stones. This simple structure can provide basic shelter and protection in a survival situation, and it can be set up quickly and easily to help you to stay warm and dry in the wild.

HYGIENE PROJECTS

Hygiene Projects

Hygiene is the practice of maintaining cleanliness and health in the body, surroundings, and objects that come in contact with the body. Basic hygiene is paramount to staying healthy. In a survival situation, the importance of good hygiene becomes even more critical, as access to modern amenities such as running water may be limited or non-existent. Without health, nothing else matters. In this section, I have a few projects to help your no-grid lifestyle be a little more pathogen-free.

How To Build A Dirt-Cheap Composting Toilet

Difficulty: Easy

One of the most important inventions in the world is modern plumbing. Some historians say this saved more people throughout human history than doctors have! Having a working toilet is more than just a luxury; it's preventative healthcare. When the grid goes down, you need a way of getting rid of your human biowaste and sewage. Now there are many ways you could deal with sewage, but I'm not going to cover the elegant solution. I will cover the solution you could assemble in 5 minutes with basic supplies from any hardware store. Enter the composting toilet.

The composting toilet, you guessed it, turns human waste into compost. It doesn't require a plumbing system; it's a bucket with carbon-rich materials like sawdust or peat moss, so bacteria have the right balance of carbon and nitrogen materials to decompose waste.

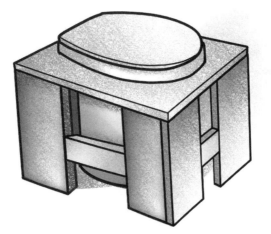

Materials

- ☐ Five-gallon bucket
- ☐ 2x4 planks of wood (should be the same length as the bucket)
- ☐ Large plywood sheet
- ☐ Toilet seat lid
- ☐ Screws

Steps

1. Cut a hole the size and shape of the bucket in the plywood sheet.

2. Drill holes for the toilet seat into the plywood.

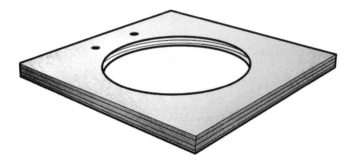

3. Screw 2 2x4's together into an L shape to be the legs of the toilet. You should do this four times so you have four legs.

4. Screw them to the bottom corners of the plywood sheet.

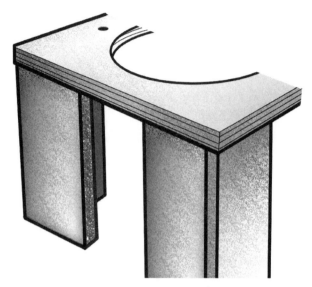

5. Add some horizontal supports, so the legs stay straight.

6. Make sure it stands solidly on its own.

7. Put the bin underneath.

How To Use

1. Add absorbent material: sawdust, dead leaves, newspaper, etc.

2. Poop and pee in it. Toilet paper is fine to keep in there. If a strong smell lingers, you need to add more absorbent material.

3. Empty into the compost pile every 4-5 days.

4. Let the human waste sit in the compost pile for at least a year before using it in your garden. It is not safe to introduce manure to your garden immediately as it may contain disease-containing pathogens or dangerous

metabolites of medication.

Pro tip: Use water instead of toilet paper for cleanup. You can make a DIY bidet by getting a plastic water bottle and poking holes in the top. The pressure from squeezing the bottle will help you clean up without toilet paper.

How To Build A Simple Bucket Washing Machine

Difficulty: Easy

Just because SHTF doesn't mean you should neglect basic hygiene. Maintaining a hygiene standard is important for maintaining a sense of normalcy and supporting long-term health. A bucket washing system is one of the easiest ways to do laundry without depending on a washing machine or electricity. This method also saves a lot of water.

Materials

- ☐ Two 5-gallon buckets (Must have a handle)
- ☐ Plunger

Tools

- ☐ Power drill
- ☐ Half-inch drill bit

Steps

1. Drill evenly distributed holes on the bottom of the bucket using the half-inch drill bit. Repeat for the sides of the lower half of the bucket.

2. Drill a few holes through the rubber of the plunger.

3. Insert the drilled bucket into the normal bucket and insert the plunger. Your setup is now ready for your first round of laundry.

How To Do Laundry

1. Put clothes into the bucket washing machine.

2. Put water and detergent in the bucket washing machine

3. Move the plunger up and down for a few minutes.

4. Pick up the drain basket and put it into a bucket of clean water to rinse. If you need to do multiple loads, I recommend having a bottom bucket to hold soapy water and a bottom bucket to hold clean water. If you don't want to get a third bucket, you can simply pour out the soapy water and fill it with clean water.

5. Pick up the drain basket and spin it to remove excess water after the clothes are rinsed. You can hang dry the clothes afterward.

How To Do Laundry Just Like Grandma Used To

Difficulty: Medium

This project is a good alternative to the bucket/plunger washer, but it will require a little extra engineering to pull off. The idea is to create a hand-powered rotating chamber for your clothes.

Materials

- □ Large rectangular plastic bin (Must have high sides because it will hold water)

- □ 2 Plastic mesh bins

- □ 2-inch PVC pipe (Longer than the length of your large washing basin)

- □ 2 PVC 90° bend

- □ PVC end cap

- ☐ PVC glue

- ☐ Cable ties

- ☐ Yarn or twine

Tools

- ☐ Drill

- ☐ 2-inch hole saw drill bit

- ☐ Scissors

- ☐ Soldering iron

Steps

1. Drill a 2-inch circular hole through the bottom of your bathroom bins.

2. Join the two bathroom bins together; their rims should face each other and be secured tightly with cable ties. The holes drilled on their bases should be facing opposite directions.

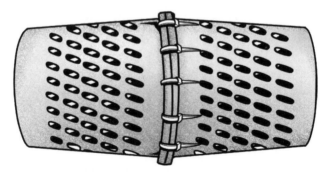

3. Place the conjoined bathroom bins in the main rectangular washing basin with their drilled bottoms facing t's width (shorter sides). The conjoined bathroom bins should not touch the bottom of the washing basin.

Use this as a reference when marking the point where you will drill two extra 2-inch holes: a hole on each side along the width of the basin. The PVC pipe will go through these holes and act as an axle.

4.   Drill using the 2-inch hole saw bit at the marked area from step 3.

5.   Slide the PVC pipe through one of the holes we drilled on the basin, push it through the joined bathroom bins, and out the other end of the basin. The bathroom bins should be hanging in the center of the basin without touching the bottom but still adequately contained within the larger basin.

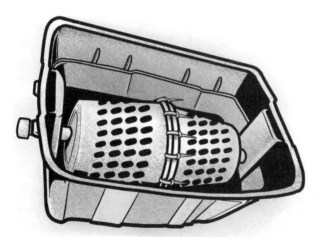

6. Attach the end cap to one side of the container using PVC glue and allow enough time to set.

7. Attach the two PVC bends on the other end to create a handle.

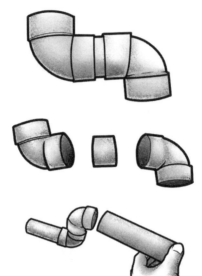

8. Use scissors to cut open a small 'door' through the joined bathroom bins; this is where you put your clothes.

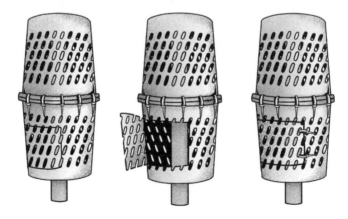

9. Use the soldering iron to poke a hole through the part of the PVC pipe between the basin wall and the bathroom

bin (On the side nearest to the handle). Run the twine through this hole and tie it to the bathroom bin. This string binds the bin to the PVC pipe and ensures they spin together.

You now have a manual hand-powered spinning washer. When using this method (or the Bucket/plunger combo), I recommend soaking the laundry in detergent for a couple of hours first. This helps reduce the energy you will spend manually washing your load, as the dirt, scum, sweat, and grime is loosened up before the workout you'll get when doing laundry.

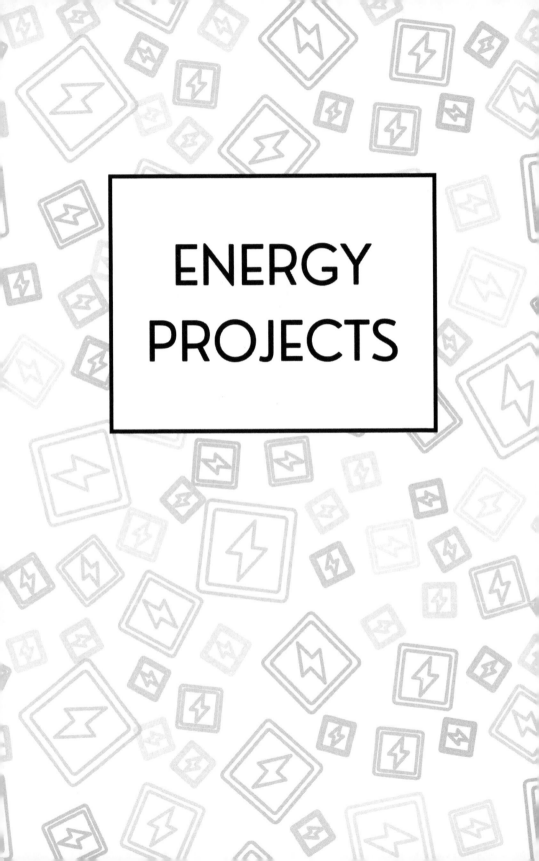

ENERGY PROJECTS

Energy Projects

During a no-grid crisis, having access to energy can be crucial for survival. It can be used to power essential equipment and devices, such as lights, medical equipment, and communication devices. It can also be used for cooking, heating, and other basic needs. Having a reliable source of energy can make a significant difference in a the outcome of a crisis. DIY energy projects can provide a way to generate your own heat and power when you can't rely on the grid. These projects can be relatively simple to construct and can be a cost-effective way to ensure that you have access to energy when you need it the most.

The Basic Solar Setup

Difficulty: Hard

There are many ways to get your power, but those options are severely limited in a no grid situation. I've long been a proponent of solar, and for good reason. We are orbiting an enormous fusion reactor in space that beams huge quantities of energy straight to earth. Why not use it? The beauty of solar energy is that it is sustainable and independent. An important aspect of being prepared is self-reliance. When you learn how to tap into the power of the sun, you are no longer bound by the need for external infrastructure for your basic electricity needs. A grid-down scenario becomes less worrisome when you have an unlimited source of power that appears every day for free. Granted, a system that can power every device or appliance in your household will not be affordable for most people. However, you can still select a few crucial devices/appliances and design a system that can cater to their daily energy consumption.

Building your own solar setup may seem complex and unapproachable. However, this section is meant to break the complexity down to the basics and help you design a system that will work for your individual needs or requirements.

Step 1: Energy Consumption

Every household or individual consumes varying amounts of electricity per day through their appliances, tools, and personal tech. When designing your solar system, the first step is to determine how much energy you consume. This will not only help you determine the necessary capacity and specifications of your system, but also its cost.

Every electric-powered appliance, tool, or device has a wattage. You can find this information on the product itself or its packaging. Alternatively, you can use a watt meter to measure the wattage yourself. For the purposes of this explanation, I will refer to all appliances, tools, and tech products as "devices."

Once you know the wattage of your devices, you need to determine the quantity (if there is more than one), and how many hours they will be running per day. For example, if you have 5 LED bulbs that consume 6 watts each and run for 5 hours a day:

> 5 LED bulbs x 6 Watts/bulb x 5 hours/day = 150 watt-hours/day

To calculate the total watt-hours or Wh per day, you need to do this for each device in your household. Once you have the total watt-hours per day, you can use this information to determine the size and specifications of your solar system.

 Keep in mind that if you plan to power high-wattage devices like electric stoves, large fridges, and air conditioners, this will significantly raise the cost of your system. If you have trouble calculating the values, a variety of online calculators are available to help you complete this step.

When calculating your daily energy consumption, you will use the simple formula above for each category of device. Once you have the necessary values, you will add them up to get the sum total of watt-hours consumed daily. Refer to the following table for an example of how to calculate energy usage for multiple devices.

Device	No. Devices	Consump (W)	Time Used (Hr)	Total Usage (W-Hr)
LED Bulb	5	6	5	150
Television	1	60	5	300
Laptop	1	40	5	200
Total				**650**

Note: Figures will vary depending on the specifications of individual products.

If you're designing a system that will power everything in your home, you can simply check your energy bill, which will show you how much electricity you consume. The average US household consumes 30 kilowatt hours a day (or 30,000 watt-hours).

Step 2: Battery Selection

Before I start this section, you should know that you don't actually need a battery. Batteries are a significant cost of the solar system, sometimes even the largest expense. If you plan to only use your electrical appliances during the day AND are not using more power than your system can put out at once, you may not need a battery at all.

For example, if you're just interested in having a couple of panels so you can charge a few phones during the day, then you are totally good to skip out on including a battery. In that case, I would get a 20,000 mAh power bank (which costs less than $30 on Amazon) and use that as my battery. It won't be able to power any energy-hungry devices like a TV, but it can charge your phone/tablet and other small electronic devices just fine. I've even been able to charge my laptop from a power bank. It's slow, and will still drain if you're using it while charging, but it works!

However, if you want your solar system to be stable and consistent (don't want the TV to turn off when a cloud passes overhead) and power your devices at night or during periods of low sunlight, a larger battery is necessary.

When choosing a battery for your solar system, there are several factors to consider. The first is the type of battery. There are two main types of batteries: lead-acid and lithium-ion. Lead-acid batteries are less expensive but also heavier and require more maintenance. Lithium-ion batteries are more expensive but are lighter, last longer, and require less maintenance.

The second thing to consider is the battery's capacity. The size of the battery you need will depend on how much energy you need to store and how long you need to be able to use it. This is usually measured in ampere-hours (Ah).

Next is the battery's voltage, which should match the voltage of your solar panels and inverter. Batteries are rated by two main specifications: ampere-hours (Ah) and voltage (V). To determine the size of battery you need for your solar system, you can use the following formula:

$$C = T / (V \times 0.5)$$
C = Capacity Needed (Ah)
T = Total Daily Energy Consumption (W-Hr) (From step 1)
V = Battery Voltage (V)

For example, if you have a daily energy consumption of 650 watt-hours and you are using a 12V battery:

Capacity needed (Ah) = 650 / (12 * 0.5) = 108 Ah

In this case, you would need a battery with a capacity of at least 108 Ah. The nearest-sized battery that you can find that would work for this design is a 120 Ah/12V battery. This will cost around $250 - $400, depending on the brand you choose.

This is for a lead-acid battery, as you generally don't want to go under 50% charge to preserve the battery's life. If you are using a lithium-ion battery, you can divide by 0.8 instead, so the calculation would be:

Capacity needed (Ah) = 650 / (12 * 0.8) = 68 Ah

If you're like most people, your daily energy consumption will require you to have multiple batteries in your system, as one just won't cut it. There are two ways to connect multiple batteries together: in series or in parallel. Batteries wired in series will have their voltages added, while those wired in parallel will maintain the same voltage, but increase in capacity (Ah). Either way, both configurations result in the same total energy (which is measured in watt-hours).

Your decision to wire in parallel vs series depends on your system capacity and the voltage of your solar charge controller and panel. If you're using 12v panels and a 12v solar charge controller, then you would wire in parallel to maintain the same voltage.

To connect in parallel you would connect the positive end of one battery to the positive end of the next, and the negative to the negative. To connect in series, you would connect the positive end of one battery to the negative of the next battery, and the negative to the positive.

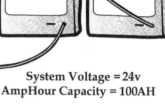

Batteries In Parallel

**Voltage remains the same
AmpHour capacity doubles**

12V
100AH

12V
100AH

System Voltage = 12v
AmpHour Capacity = 200AH

Batteries In Series

**Voltage doubles
AmpHour capacity
stays the same**

12V
100AH

12V
100AH

System Voltage = 24v
AmpHour Capacity = 100AH

Step 3: Selecting Appropriate Solar Panels

To choose the right solar panels for your off-grid solar system, you'll need to consider three main factors: daily energy consumption, peak sun hours, and panel efficiency. First, determine your daily energy consumption and the size of the battery you'll need to store that energy (steps 1 and 2 above). Next, consider the peak sun hours in your area, which is the amount of time each day when the sun's rays are strongest. You can use a solar resource map online to get an idea of the peak sun hours in your area. Finally, consider the efficiency of the solar panels you're considering. Monocrystalline panels are typically more efficient than polycrystalline panels, but they are also more expensive. Most modern monocrystalline solar panels have an efficiency of around 18-24%. This number represents the total solar energy that is captured in that area. This may sound low, but it's important to keep in mind that the theoretical limit for a single-junction silicon monocrystalline cell (the type of panel that is most commonly used) is around 32%. This is known as the Shockley-Queisser limit.

To calculate the wattage of the solar panels you need, use the following formula:

$$W = T / (H \times E)$$

W = Panel Wattage (W)

T = Total Daily Energy Consumption (Wh)

H = Peak Sun Hours

E = System Efficiency

For example, if your daily energy consumption is 650 watt-hours and you have an average of 5 peak sun hours per day with a system efficiency of 70%, you would need a panel wattage of 185 watts.

Panel wattage = 650 Wh / (5h * 0.7) = 185 watts

When selecting your solar panels, make sure to choose a reputable brand and ensure that the panel voltage is the same as, or at least 20-30% higher than, your battery voltage. This will help ensure that your system is reliable and efficient.

We use a system efficiency of 70% because your conditions won't always be perfect, and your panels won't be able to capture 100% of their rated energy. This factor accounts for any potential losses due to factors such as dust, shade, or temperature. By using a lower efficiency value in your calculation, you can ensure that your panels will be able to meet your energy needs even on less-than-ideal days.

For the example above, a single 200-watt/12V solar panel would be sufficient and will run you around $200.

If you would like to connect multiple solar panels together, the same principles of series and parallel connection apply here. To connect in parallel you would connect the positive cable of one panel to the positive of the next, and the negative to the negative. To connect in series, you would connect the positive end of one panel to the negative of the next, and the negative to the positive. Connecting in series will add up your voltages. Two 12V solar panels connected in series would produce 24V. The decision to connect in parallel or series depends on your solar charge controller and battery voltage.

Step 4: Selecting A Solar Charge Controller

A charge controller is an essential component of an off-grid solar power system. They are installed between the solar panels and the battery, regulating the flow of current and ensuring that the battery is charged safely. Charge controllers also prevent overcharging, which can significantly increase the lifespan of your battery.

There are two main types of charge controllers: pulse width modulation (PWM) and maximum power point tracking (MPPT). MPPT charge controllers are generally more efficient and can be up to 20-30% more expensive, but a PWM charge controller may be sufficient for smaller systems. If the voltage of your solar panels is significantly higher than the battery voltage, you may want to consider an MPPT charge controller.

To determine the size of the charge controller you need, use the following calculation:

$$R = W / V \, x \, 1.3$$

R = Charge Controller Rating (Amps)

W = Solar Panel Wattage (W)

V = Battery Voltage (V)

For example, if you have a 200-watt solar panel and a 12-volt battery, you would need a charge controller with a rating of at least 21.6 amps:

(200W / 12V) * 1.3 = 21.6 A

It's usually a good idea to choose a charge controller with a slightly higher amp rating than what you calculate, so in this case, you may want to choose a 30 amp charge controller or higher. If the charge controller has a higher amp rating than what is strictly necessary, it can handle larger variations in the flow of electricity without being overwhelmed or shutting down. This can help prevent damage to the battery and other components of the solar system, and can ensure that the battery is charged efficiently and safely.

Another reason to choose a charge controller with a higher amp rating is that it can provide extra capacity for future expansion of your solar system. If you add more solar panels or a larger battery to your system in the future, a higher-rated charge controller can handle the increased flow of electricity without needing to be replaced.

Step 5: Inverter

An inverter is a device that converts the direct current (DC) electricity produced by the solar panel into alternating current (AC) electricity, which is the type of electricity used in homes. Now, like I mentioned earlier, if you are just planning on using this panel to charge a couple of phones and power banks, you can skip this step! A standard 30A solar charge controller would have a couple of USB ports you can plug directly into.

Most electronic devices, including phones, power banks, laptops, tablets, radios, TV's, and LED lights, actually use DC power. This is why your laptop charger isn't just a cable, but has a 'brick' in it. This "brick" is an adaptor that converts the AC power from your wall socket into DC power that your laptop can use to charge. If you plan to use your laptop's charger, it takes AC power, and therfore you will need an inverter. However, you can charge a laptop (very slowly) from a power bank.

As a rule of thumb, if you can charge it with a simple USB cable, then you don't need an inverter.

An inverter is an essential component of a solar panel system, especially for large-scale installations. Inverters convert the direct current (DC) electricity produced by solar panels into alternating current (AC) electricity, which is the type of electricity typically used in households and buildings. There are two main types of inverters: modified sine wave (MSW) and pure sine wave (PSW).

PSW inverters are generally considered the better option because they produce AC electricity with a pure sine waveform, which is the same as the AC electricity supplied by utility companies. This makes PSW inverters suitable for use with a wide range of devices, including sensitive electronic equipment. In contrast, MSW inverters produce a modified sine waveform, which can cause problems for some devices. While PSW inverters are more expensive than MSW inverters, they are worth the extra cost to avoid potential damage to your equipment.

When selecting an inverter for your solar panel system, you should consider its continuous output power and surge wattage. The continuous output power tells you how many AC loads the inverter can support simultaneously, while the surge wattage indicates the maximum wattage the inverter can handle for short periods of time (such as when starting an electric motor). For example, if you need to power a 650 watt load, you would need an inverter with a continuous output power of at least 700 watts to allow for surges in power consumption. It's important not to skimp on your inverter, as a low-quality inverter can damage your entire solar panel system.

Wiring Diagram

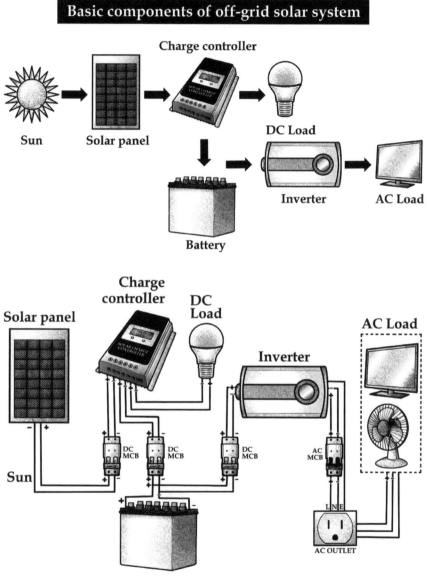

Basic components of off-grid solar system

Now that you know the essential components and their respective sizes/ratings for your own needs, you can use the above wiring diagram as a reference for how they all come together. In addition to the main equipment, you will also need:

- □ PV wiring cables (of the gauge you need)
- □ Breakers
- □ Pair of solar extension cables
- □ MC4 ring connectors (smaller batteries typically need ¼" ring connectors, larger batteries typically require ⅜" ring connectors)
- □ Heat shrink tubing

Helpful Tools

- □ Wire scraper
- □ Crimper
- □ Flat head screwdriver
- □ Pliers
- □ Drill (for mounting equipment)
- □ Socket wrench

Wire Selection And Installation

Connecting all the components of your solar system is called stringing. The size of your wire should be determined by the current carrying capacity of your design. If your wire is too small to handle the current running in the circuit, it may overheat, which can cause a potential fire. Additionally, using wires unsuitable for your system's current carrying capacity is a code violation in many jurisdictions.

Keep in mind that the longer the wire, the more resistance, which leads to increased heat and loss of energy. It is good practice to trim any excess wire between the different components in the system in order to prevent any unnecessary losses of power.

Typically, wire size in the US is denoted by the American wire gauge or AWG. The smaller the AWG specification, the more current it can handle. This means that a 10 gauge wire is a larger diameter and can handle more current than 12 gauge. You can use an online calculator that will tell you, based on your voltage, current, and wire length, which wire size you should use: www. renvu.com/solar-wire-size-calculator

In step 4, we calculated the amount of current passing through our system in order to inform the capacity of the charge controller. That amperage can also be used to inform our wire size. As a general rule of thumb, 10 gauge wire is good for up to 30 amps, while 12 gauge is good for 20 amps. Therefore, our design will use a 10 gauge wire.

Connecting the charge controller to the battery.

1. Install an MC4 ring connector to one end of each individual cable. Use a wire scraper to trim off about a ¼ inch of insulation material to expose the internal wire. Twist and insert the exposed wire through the ring connector and use the crimper or pliers to squeeze the connection together. Cover the connection with heat shrink tubing for extra insulation. This end of the cable will eventually be secured to the battery.

2. The other end of your cables will be connected to the charge controller. There will be a clear battery icon with a positive and negative inlet. Strip off a ¼ inch of insulation material from both ends, slightly twist the exposed wires, and insert one of them into the negative inlet and the other into the positive inlet. Use a flathead screwdriver to tighten the connection inside the charge controller. Typically, black cables connect negative terminals, and red cables connect positive terminals.

3. Once your cables are tightly screwed to the charge controller, they can be connected to the battery. Start with the negative, then the positive. Simply unscrew the bolt in the battery terminal, insert the ring connector through it, and screw them back together tightly into the battery terminal. You may need a socket wrench or pliers.

4. At this point, your charge controller should register the battery and display the voltage.

Solar charge controller

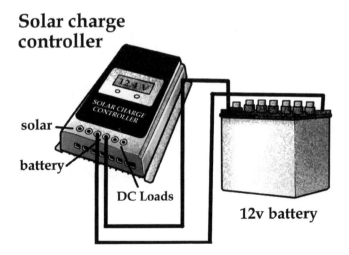

solar

battery

DC Loads

12v battery

Connecting the solar panel to the charge controller.

---

1. Cover your solar panel with a dark opaque cloth to block solar radiation and avoid electric shock during installation.

2. The cables coming out of your solar panel's junction box have connectors at the end; these are meant to be joined to the solar extension cables. The industry standard uses an mc4 connection.

3. This is typically going to be the longest string in the system, and the length of the extension cable should be informed by the distance between the panel and charge controller (or where they will be mounted).

4. The opposite ends of the solar extension cables should be connected to the charge controller by trimming off ¼ inches off the insulating material from both ends and inserting them into their respective positive and negative inlets (guided by the solar panel icon on the charge controller). Start with the negative wire and then the positive. Don't forget to screw tightly into the charge controller.

5. Place the panel in sunlight and see if the charge controller has started registering some voltage going inside the battery.

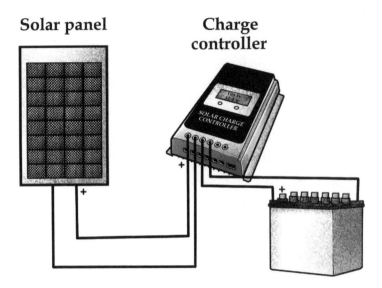

Solar panel   **Charge controller**

Connecting the inverter to the battery

1. Now that we have confirmed our panel, charge controller, and battery are in good working order, it is time to connect the inverter.

2. To add the inverter to the system, we must first undo the solar panel's connection to the charge controller for safety. Starting with the positive inlet and then followed by the negative.

3. Once the panel is disconnected from the charge controller, the inverter can be connected to the battery. Inverters come with their own cables that have ring connectors attached. First fasten the ring connector of each wire to the terminals of your inverter (Red cable to positive and black cable to negative for consistency).

4. Once the wires are fastened tightly to the inverter's terminals, they can now be connected to the battery, starting with the negative. Unscrew the bolt on the

negative terminal of your battery and insert the inverter's ring connector through it, where it will be joining the ring connector we installed previously (Coming from the charge controller). Screw them all tightly and repeat the same process for the battery's positive terminal. Use a socket wrench to tighten.

5. Plug the solar panel back into the charge controller, starting with the negative.

6. Turn on the inverter and use it to power your devices/ appliances.

This is what is needed for a basic off-grid solar system. All that is needed is to mount your panels in an appropriate location, facing the sun, where there is no interference or shade.

The Super-Duper Simple and Inexpensive Solar Build

Difficulty: Easy

Now, you should have all the information, knowledge, and instructions to build your own solar system. The only thing left to do is to actually build one. Here is an example build for an inexpensive off-grid setup that doesn't use an inverter or battery. Once you have the parts, this will only take you a few minutes to setup - no tools or expertise needed.

My goal for this project is to have some redundancy and backup in an extended no-grid situation so I can charge essential devices. My secondary goal is to not spend too much money!

With this system, I can charge/power some power banks, phones, smartwatches, electric shavers, rechargeable flashlights, radios, and other small devices (not all at the same time!)

Specifications

- □ One 200W solar panel = $195
- □ Two 20,000 mAh usb power banks $28 x 2 power banks = $56
- □ One 30A solar charge controller = $45

Total cost: $296

Setting this up couldn't be simpler. I didn't mount anything so as to leave the system portable.

1. Lay a tarp or other protective material on your floor.

2. Place your solar panel on the tarp, propped up to about 30-45 degrees using some bricks, facing south. There are many websites that will tell you the optimal angle and direction to position your panels for your location. This will change in the summer and winter, so you can add or remove bricks to adjust the angle throughout the year.

3. Connect the positive and negative wires from the solar panel to the appropriate sockets in the solar charge controller.

4. Plug a power bank into the usb port on the solar charge controller.

5. To protect the solar charge controller and power bank from the elements, place them inside a waterproof container such as a small Tupperware box. Cut a hole in the side of the box that is just big enough for the cables to pass through. This will allow the cables to connect to the charge controller and power bank, while still keeping them protected from the weather.

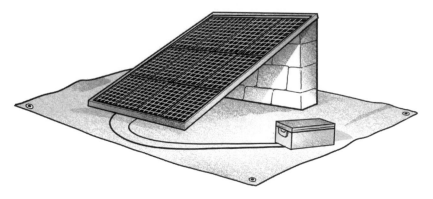

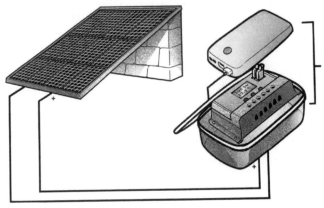

powerbank &
solar charge
controller
inside the box

How To Extract Energy From Dead Batteries And Charge Your Phone

Difficulty: Easy

In a grid-down situation, batteries may be one of the only stored energy sources. If a person can find a way to extract energy from those batteries, they may be able to power essential devices and communications equipment. Your best option for long-term power generation is solar and batteries. However, if you're in a situation where you need just a little bit of juice and have some old batteries lying around, you may be in luck.

First, a little electrical engineering. Standard AA or AAA batteries are rated at 1.5V. This is the voltage they output when "fresh." When the batteries "die," they're not actually completely depleted of chemical energy. A dead battery usually sees a drop in voltage to around 1 - 1.3V. Your device stops working because the voltage from the battery is too low to power it, and that's when you throw the batteries out and get new ones. There is a little chemical energy left in there that you can extract.

You can connect batteries in a series or parallel configuration. In a series connection, the batteries are connected end-to-end, so the voltage of the system is the sum of the voltages of the individual batteries. In a parallel connection, the batteries are connected side-by-side, so the voltage of the system is the same as the voltage of the individual batteries.

If you no longer have working batteries, you can use them to power a device by connecting them in series. To do this, you will need to connect the first battery's positive terminal to the second battery's negative terminal. Repeat this process for each additional battery until you get the required voltage.

Let's say you want to charge your phone. Modern phones require 5V to charge. You can probably get away with 4.5V or a little less. Some phones have advanced battery cells that support fast charging, in which case they may handle higher voltages. Don't worry if you give it a bit more voltage than needed, say 6V instead of 5V. Phones have internal circuits that manage power distribution; this shouldn't be a problem.

Let's assume your dead AA batteries are around 1.2 volts each. This means if you connect 4 of the batteries in series, your total voltage will be 1.2V * 4 = 4.8V, which should be enough to charge your phone.

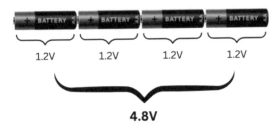

How To Connect The Batteries In Series

There are a couple of ways you do this.

The easiest way is to line them up end to end, as shown in the picture above. This should work fine as long as they touch, although it may be a bit finicky.

Alternatively, you can connect them using any conductive material. Aluminum foil works great in a pinch. Make sure to connect them as written above, positive to negative. Battery packs work great for keeping a solid connection.

How To Charge Your Phone

You may have noticed that there isn't a conveniently located USB port on these batteries to plug into. To charge, we will have to disassemble a phone charger to get the positive and negative wires.

1. Take your standard USB or wall phone charger, and snip off the end that contains either the USB or the wall brick.

2. Strip a few inches of the plastic insulating cover to expose the wires underneath. There should be a few individually wrapped wires inside.

3. If your charger conforms to international standards, the wires will be color coded. Strip a ½" of plastic covering off the red and black wires. Connect the red wire to the positive end of your battery and the black to the negative. Move the other wires out of the way, and don't let them touch.

4. Plug your phone into the other end and watch it light up.

This will work great in a pinch, but don't expect to get lots of juice out of dead batteries.

How To Make Charcoal

Difficulty: Easy

Think of charcoal as purified wood. Charcoal burns faster and hotter than wood, with the added benefit of not producing much smoke. A pyrolysis chemical reaction breaks down many of the complex compounds in the wood into compounds that will burn much cleaner.

Materials

- ☐ Hardwood
- ☐ Metal barrel with lid
- ☐ Kindling
- ☐ Metal poker

Steps

1. Start a fire in the barrel with the kindling and some wood. Make sure the heat builds up.

2. Add some hardwood and allow it to blacken before adding more.

3. Once all the hardwood begins burning and blackening, put the lid on the barrel.

4. Let the wood smolder for 24 hours.

5. Check on the wood to make sure it is finished smoldering. If not, give it a few more hours.

6. Remove the black wood from the barrel. Congratulations, you now have charcoal!

Charcoal has almost double the energy density of wood, so it's a great way to stock up on fuel in a space-efficient manner.

How To Store Fuel

Difficulty: Easy

You may want to power things like an emergency generator or your vehicle during a SHTF event. For example, a hurricane may disrupt supply lines for extended periods.

Flammable fuels like gasoline, diesel, or propane need special consideration for storage.

The first thing is to find out your area's local regulations and fire codes. Depending on the jurisdiction, there are limits to how much fuel you can typically store. Additionally, reviewing your insurance coverage for liability issues may be wise.

It is not recommended to store emergency gas in plastic containers, especially long-term. The typical red jerry can with thin walls just won't cut it. Real metal jerry cans are typically expensive but well worth the cost as long-term containers. They are not prone to expansion and cracking like plastic jerry cans. Metal resists expansion and prevents any vapors from leaking.

You do not want to expose your family to any leaked fumes. This is why experts recommend that any flammable fuel source be stored away from the house; an outdoor shed or detached garage is a safer location. Irresponsible gasoline storage is hazardous, especially when using cheap plastic.

Preppers should be extra safety-conscious. If the vapor leaks and makes its way to any spark, like a gas furnace or water heater, you could be facing an explosive disaster. You should generally store fuel in a cool, dry place away from the house.

Different fuels have different shelf lives. The typical gasoline you get from the pump will usually deteriorate within three months inside your gas tank. If you store it in a sealed gasoline-approved container, it can last up to 6 months. Adding fuel stabilizers like STA-BIL to the gasoline could extend its life for an extra 1-2 years. Typically, ethanol-free gas lasts longer than the E10 gas (10% ethanol) widely available in the US.

Diesel generally keeps much better than gasoline and can last up to 12 months when stored in an appropriate diesel metal jerry can. If you plan to store it for a longer period, you will need to mix some fuel stabilizers and biocides.

Whether you store diesel or gas will depend on what your vehicle or generator drinks. It is ideal to have some uniformity to avoid storing different types of fuel, as well as to make rotation easier.

Stored gasoline or diesel should be cycled regularly. It's nice to store stabilized fuel in good containers, but why let it go to waste? Whenever your car needs gas and the urge strikes, you can use the stored fuel to refill and replace it with fresh gas. Rotation is important to avoid waste and disposal.

Another thing to consider is a dual-fuel generator, which can help avoid reliance on one fuel type. They allow for the option of using propane, which is more expensive but will store for decades and is one of the most stable, efficient, and reliable fuel sources.

How To Build A Fuel-Efficient Rocket Stove

Difficulty: Medium

There are many ways to build a rocket stove because the principle behind it is very straightforward. In this project, we will be using cans. This project essentially recycles common materials you're probably storing in the pantry.

The main idea of a rocket stove is to build an 'L' shaped hollow passage that allows air to flow from the bottom to burn fuel at the base and release heat from the top, which can then be used for cooking or basic warmth.

Materials

- [ ] One large empty No. 10 can (They are approximately 6¼ inches tall and 7 inches in diameter)

- [ ] 2 medium-sized number No. 300 cans (About 4 inches tall and 3 inches in diameter)

- [ ] A smaller-sized soup can (12-14 oz)

- [ ] A bucket

- [ ] Plaster

- [ ] Sand

- [ ] Perlite

- [ ] Water

Tools

- ☐ Drill
- ☐ Dremel or Tin snips
- ☐ Marker
- ☐ Round file

Directions

1. The large No.10 can will be the main body of the rocket stove. The first step is to cut a circle roughly a quarter inch above the can's base. Use the soup can as a stencil because its diameter will eventually fill this hole. Use the drill to poke holes around the circumference. The holes make it easier when using the Dremel/ tin strips to finish the cut.

2. Use the round file to smoothen out any serrations left behind in the cutting process.

3. Use the soup can again to trace another hole into the medium-sized no. 300 can. Cut using the same method in

step 1.

4. Cut the base of the soup can off. Place the medium-sized can into the large can. Push the soup can through both holes into the center of the nested cans. Make sure it can fit snugly through both medium and large cans.

5. Cut the bottom of the other medium-sized can off and cut the can vertically so you have a round metal sheet. Insert it into the medium can in the stove's center. Push it down or trim it so it sits about an inch underneath the rim of the big can.

6. Cut a hole on the lid of the large can using the medium-sized can as a stencil. This will be the roof of your chimney.

7. Use the Dremel or tin strips to cut out a couple of tabs that you can later bend to secure the lid after adding the insulating medium. The cuts should be approximately half an inch into the top.

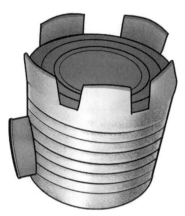

8. The recommended insulating mixture should consist of ½ plaster, ¼ perlite, and ¼ sand. However, you can always use whatever is readily available, including gravel or pebbles. The mixture helps hold everything together and gives our rocket stove a bit of weight.

9. Use a bucket to mix and add water until it reaches a cake batter consistency.

10. Carefully fill the hollow spaces between the walls of the medium can and the larger can. Place a cover on the chimney to avoid getting the insulating mix inside. Keep in mind that this mixture settles quickly, so get this step done before it solidifies.

11. Place the lid of the larger can to cover the mixture. Make sure the medium-sized can is centered to align with the lid's hole. You now have a rocket stove.

12. Bend down the tabs we cut earlier to hold the lid in place.

Ignite sticks or twigs to fuel your rocket stove. Additionally, consider getting some expanded mesh on the stove when cooking/ heating smaller pots or cans.

How To Build A Solar Oven

Difficulty: Medium

If you've ever played with a magnifying glass as a kid, you probably understand the principle of a solar cooker, turning light energy into heat. There are many ways to build a solar cooker, and this section will explain how to make a basic setup that works as long as there is adequate sunlight. Keep in mind that solar cookers are typically very slow, and if you're using them for cooking meat, make sure the temperature (of the meat) has reached at least 170 degrees Fahrenheit, which is the point at which germs are killed.

Materials

- ☐ Aluminum foil
- ☐ Four sticks
- ☐ Glue
- ☐ Torn fabric or shredded newspaper
- ☐ Cardboard
- ☐ 2 cubic cardboard boxes (one larger than the other)
- ☐ Black construction paper

Tools

- ☐ Utility knife
- ☐ Measuring tape
- ☐ Duct tape

Steps

1. Use the utility knife to cut off the tops of the cardboard boxes.

2. Place the smaller box inside the larger one, and use glue on its base to position it in the center of the larger box. Ideally, there should be at least an inch of space between the walls of the two boxes.

3. Fill the space between the walls with shredded paper or torn fabric to act as an insulating layer that will later trap the heat. Stuff the shredded paper adequately until the top.

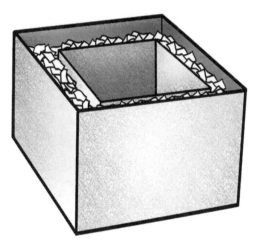

4. Measure the dimensions of the inner box to cut the black construction paper to size. Use glue to attach/line the smaller box with the construction paper. The black color retains and absorbs heat more efficiently.

5. Measure the width of the larger box. This will be used when cutting a trapezoidal shape from the cardboard, where one face will be the width of the large box and the

opposite face approximately 2 inches longer. You will need four trapezoidal cardboard cutouts.

6. Cover the surface of the trapezoidal cut-outs with aluminum foil and ensure it is glued as smoothly as possible. Avoid making any wrinkles.

7. Use duct tape to attach the cut-outs along the width of your large box. At this point, you have a smaller cardboard box inside the larger one, with trapezoidal aluminum flaps duck taped to the top of the larger box.

8. Use the sticks to prop up the flaps at around a 45-degree angle to capture and concentrate the sun's light into the cooker.

This basic solar cooker can save you during a crisis when the grid goes down, and there is no alternative fuel source. If you live in an area with enough sunlight, using the sun's free energy to cook is viable as long as there is enough sunlight (peak hours are generally between 11 am and 2 pm).

As mentioned earlier, this method cooks slowly, and you must ensure that your food has been thoroughly cooked from the inside before eating. Use caution because uncooked food can lead to food poisoning, which is the last thing you need when SHTF.

Water Heating Projects

Even if you're not in a no-grid situation, there are many reasons why it would be a good idea to build a solar water heater. First, solar water heaters can save you a significant amount of money on energy bills. They are very efficient at converting the energy from sunlight into a nice hot shower. You can build one with relative ease for a low cost, and they can last for many years with proper maintenance.

Here's a quick primer on how a solar heater works if you're out of the loop. Solar water heaters are devices that use solar energy (sunlight) to generate heat, typically used to heat water. They usually consist of a solar collector and a storage tank. The solar collector is a device that absorbs solar radiation and transfers it to the water, which is recirculated into the tank. These solar collectors are usually a simple set of pipes that water runs through.

We are trying to accomplish two main things with a solar water heater. The first is to maximize the amount of sunlight that is hitting our solar collector. The second is to minimize the heat escaping from the heated water into the environment. For best results, you will need to insulate your pipes, the box holding your setup, and the water tank.

Commercial water heaters can cost thousands of dollars and often use a mix of water and antifreeze in the pipes that get heated before transferring that heat to the clean water in your tank. However, this build is significantly more complex and requires electricity to run a pump and temperature sensors. I will discuss two builds, one simple that runs off your garden hose and one more complex build that contains a water tank and can heat large volumes of water over the day.

The Dirt-Cheap Garden Hose Water Heater

Difficulty: Easy

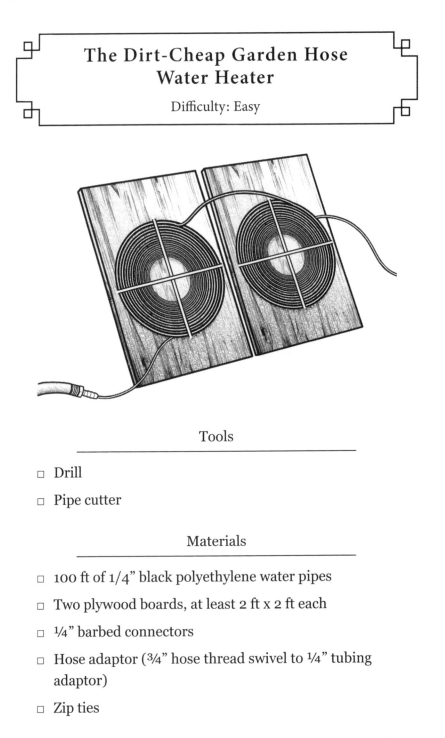

Tools

- □ Drill
- □ Pipe cutter

Materials

- □ 100 ft of 1/4" black polyethylene water pipes
- □ Two plywood boards, at least 2 ft x 2 ft each
- □ ¼" barbed connectors
- □ Hose adaptor (¾" hose thread swivel to ¼" tubing adaptor)
- □ Zip ties

□ Aluminum foil

□ Wooden dowels (I use ¼" x 12," but any size can work)

Directions

1. Choose a sunny location for your solar water heater. The location should be close to your water source and have unobstructed sunlight for most of the day.

2. Line the back of your plywood boards with aluminum foil.

3. Coil your polyethylene pipe into two tightly wound circles containing 50 ft of pipe.

4. If your pipe came as 50 ft bundles, connect the two circles with a ¼" barbed connector.

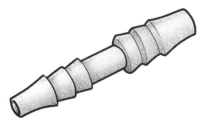

5. Place each wound circle onto the back of a plywood board. Place the wooden dowels in the + configuration shown in the image, and use a heavy-duty stapler to secure each dowel in place from the top and the bottom. If you don't have a stapler, you can use a drill to make two small holes near each dowel's top and bottom and secure them with a zip tie.

6. Attach the hose adaptor to one of the open ends of the poly pipe.

7. Place your mounted boards in the sunlight and connect

your hose adaptor to your garden hose.

8. [Optional] Rest your boards against some concrete bricks or other structure to incline them at a 30-45 degree angle, south-facing if you live in the northern hemisphere

9. Turn the garden hose on, and let water move through the system at a relatively slow pace. Collect your hot water on the other side.

With this simple build, I can get 140 degrees F on a sunny day. Of course, the disadvantages of this setup are that it requires a working garden hose, requires manual starting and stopping, doesn't have an insulated water tank reservoir, and can't recycle the water to increase temperatures.

But there is one massive benefit to it: it's dirt cheap. If you already have the needed tools, this project can cost under $50. Pretty good for what you get.

You can easily scale up this build by adding more coils. You could heat a much larger volume of water to a higher temperature if you had four or more coils.

The High Throughput Passive Solar Water Heater

Difficulty: Hard

This next build will be a little more complex and expensive but will allow you to heat up to 100 liters of water per day and take advantage of an insulated water reservoir to store and use the hot water whenever you please.

In this build, we will construct a wooden frame that holds the solar collector (the pipes). It will be insulated to reduce heat loss, and water will passively flow in and out from a water reservoir.

Part 1: Building The Casing

You will first need to build the wooden frame to house the solar collector. You can make this any size you want. For this project, I use a size of 4 ft by 4 ft.

Materials

- ☐ 1 plywood sheet (12mm x 4' x 8')
- ☐ 1 R5 rigid foam insulation sheet (1" x 4' x 8')
- ☐ 16 sqft of reflective foam
- ☐ Glue
- ☐ Screws (1")
- ☐ Waterproofing sealant for wood

Directions

1. Cut the plywood sheet into two 4' x 4' pieces, and put one piece aside; that will be the base of your collector box.

2. Take the other 4' x 4' piece and segment it into four 5.5" width pieces and four 6.5" width pieces. These will be used as the sides of the collector box. You should use the entire sheet if all the cuts are parallel.

3. Glue a 6.5" wooden piece to each side of the collector box base. Then, glue a 5.5" piece inside each edge. This will give the box a 1" lip and allow you to place a glass pane on top of it when completed.

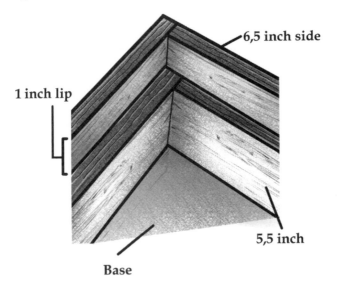

4. Add at least 2-3 layers of waterproofing sealant around the inside and outside of the box.5. Cover the inside surface of your collector box with the foam insulation sheet. Do not cover the lip you created. Glue it down.

5. Cover the insulation with reflective foam.

Part 2: The Tubes And Connections

Materials

- ☐ 6 copper pipes (1/2" x 3m)
- ☐ Two copper elbows (1/2" x 90°)
- ☐ Two copper couplings (1/2")
- ☐ 26 copper tee (1/2")
- ☐ One copper cap (1/2")
- ☐ 28 ½" pipe fasteners
- ☐ 60 1" screws
- ☐ Copper solder and paste flux
- ☐ Black spray paint (matte preferred)
- ☐ Sandpaper
- ☐ 4' x 4 metal sheet (corrugated metal or laminate metal works)

Constructing the solar collector should be straightforward using the parts list and the pictures provided. Cold water flows in the bottom right, and hot water flows out the top left.

1. Cut the copper pipes into fourteen 3.5 ft (1.07 m pieces) and twenty-eight 2.5" pieces

2. Connect the pipes as shown in the picture. It's advised to sand the outer extremities of the pipes before connecting them.

3. Once all pieces are connected and look good, solder them and test for leaks by running water through the pipes.

4. Fasten the copper pipes to the metal sheet using the ½"
    pipe fasteners along 2 points on every pipe. Screw in with
    the 1" screws.

5. Spray-paint the pipes and metal plate black. Cover it fully,
    but don't overdo it on the paint.

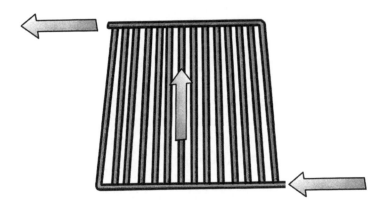

Part 3: The Water Reservoir And Finalizing

Materials

□ Six ½" pipe fasteners.

□ One clear glass pane sized to the final measurements of
  your collector box (interior). The more insulating, the
  better; a double pane will do better than a single pane.

□ Old (recycled) water heater tank - 110L or any size you can
  find (If it's cylindrical, you will have to build a small stand
  for it)

□ Fiberglass/glass wool insulation

□ Clear wrap

□ ½" PVC tubing

□ PVC glue

□ ½" PVC elbows (depends on your design)

Directions

1. Place the now-finished collector plate inside the collector box. Secure it to the insulation in the box using the pipe fasteners and screws.

2. Cut an input and output hole in the collector box for the PVC pipes to pass through. Make sure the hole is exactly the size you need. Don't leave any gaps for it to leak heat.

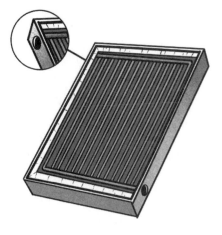

3. Connect the input PVC pipe to the lowermost valve on your water tank, and connect the output PVC pipe to the top valve on your water tank. Use elbows as needed to accommodate your tank design. Because hot water rises, this will allow the cold water from the bottom of the tank to enter the solar collector and the heated water to remain at the top of your tank.

4. Take your water heater tank and cover it in as much fiberglass insulation as possible while wrapping it with the clear wrap to hold it in place. Once secured, you can add another layer over it to improve aesthetics, such as a tarp.

5. Finally, place your glass pane on top of the collector, and seal it with waterproof silicone sealant. The tighter the fit, the better.

For positioning, you want your collector to be about 30-45 degrees off the ground, facing south (if you're in the northern hemisphere). If you're in an area where the weather gets below freezing regularly, this probably isn't the best system, as it may even get damaged if the water inside the pipes manages to freeze. Also, it may help to give it a slight horizontal tilt (2-3 degrees) to help prevent water stagnation in the horizontal pipe segments. Water stagnation can lead to scale and biofilm buildup, allowing dangerous legionella bacteria to breed and infest your water.

If you're planning on integrating this in your home, you'll need to connect the uppermost outlet on the water tank to your house's hot water line and the lowermost outlet to your house's cold water line. Otherwise, you can manually add water to the tank and retrieve hot water a couple of hours later by pulling water from the top of the tank.

MATERIAL PROJECTS

Material Projects

You may be stuck with the materials around you in a no-grid situation. Building materials can be essential for constructing a shelter and other necessary structures. These materials can help to protect you from the elements or repair crucial structures. These are typically hard to get during a no-grid situation, so learning to utilize your surroundings to create strong and durable building materials is worthwhile.

How To Process Soil Into Clay

Difficulty: Easy

There are different grades of clay. The method that I will share with you is very crude and won't produce the type of clay used in porcelain or earthenware, but it will get the job done if you need to repair your house or build a solid structure.

To find clay soil, look at river banks. Clay retains water well; you will know when you find it. Your feet will sink into it, and it's slippery. To test the soil to see if it's clay, add some water and try rolling it into a snake. If you can wrap it around your finger without breaking, then it's decent clay.

Steps

1. Mix the clay with a lot of water until it has a light consistency and can be poured.

2. Pour the clay through a sieve or cloth to remove large particles. Small stones and other imperfections will make the clay hard to work with.

3. Let the slurry sit for a day or two; the clay will settle to the bottom, and you can simply pour the water off the top.

4. Let the remaining water evaporate, or put the clay on a cloth so it can dry out.

You can now use this terracotta clay for construction, such as filling cracks and joining rocks together. Depending on the quality of your clay, you may have luck creating some rudimentary pots.

How To Make Cob Bricks

Difficulty: Easy

Cob has been used for hundreds of years in construction. Cob has excellent thermal insulation properties and is 100% natural. The materials to make it are very common.

Materials

- ☐ Clay subsoil. Keep digging past the organic layer of soil, and you'll find a dense, clayey subsoil.

- ☐ Straw fibers. You will use it to bind to the clay. The stronger, the better.

- ☐ Water

- ☐ Brick mold. You can make this out of wood scraps. It just needs to be brick-shaped.

Steps

1. Mix the clay and straw.

2. Gradually incorporate water and stomp on the mixture to keep it as homogenous as possible.

3. Let the mixture rest for a day.

4. Put cob paste into the brick mold and let it sit for a day or two.

5. Remove the cob brick and let it sit in a dry and sunny area for about two weeks.

Now you have one cob brick. A bit laborious for one brick, I'll admit.

How To Make Fire Starter From Recycled Paper

Difficulty: Easy

Paper burns well, but it burns out almost instantly, so it's not very useful for starting logs. You can transform this common kindling into a long-lasting firestarter.

Materials

☐ Paper

☐ Strainer

☐ Bucket

Steps

1. Shred the paper and let it soak in a bucket with water for a few hours.

2. Mix and break up the wet paper until it becomes like paper mache.

3. Strain the paper mixture and let it dry overnight. Sometimes water can be trapped, so mixing it around and pushing on it can help remove excess water.

4. When the mixture is dry as it can be, tear off a fist-sized amount of paper and squeeze the water out. Place it in a dry and sunny location and let the ball dry out.

5. Repeat for the rest of the paper mixture. After a couple of weeks, you will have a lot of paper firestarters.

COMMUNICATION PROJECTS

Communication Projects

Communication is important in any situation, but it is especially important in a no-grid scenario because it allows people to communicate and coordinate. Radio can help people coordinate their efforts to survive and thrive without modern infrastructure. You also want to be able to protect your vital communications equipment from potential damage.

Communicating When The Cell Towers Are Down

Everyone has a smartphone, but don't assume that cell service will always be available or that you will have access to the internet if SHTF.

A big difference between normal cellular telephone systems and radio systems is that cellular networks rely on infrastructures like towers, fiber, or base stations to work. Land mobile radio systems or personal radio devices allow point-to-point communication between users. There are two main types of radio devices:

- Receivers
- Transceivers

Receivers

As the name suggests, receivers pick up on radio frequencies and are a means for one-way communication, meaning they do not allow you to broadcast; an example would be the typical AM/FM radio. If you can't access the internet or your cellular network fails, this might be your only way to pick up on the news, weather, public alerts, and general information.

Weather radios

At the minimum, everyone should own a weather radio that can pick up NOAA weather alerts; in addition to the typical AM/FM bands, they are incredibly affordable and can be bought for next to nothing at flea markets. Modern weather radios also have automatic alert systems. If you're buying a weather radio, get one with solar or hand-crank charging capabilities. AA battery-powered radios are a good option too.

Short-wave radios

These can pick up radio signals from all over the world and will be your only way to receive international information.

Transceivers

There's a reason we don't communicate using radio technology, and it is important to know why.Privacy is never guaranteed, and you must carefully select what you say and what information you broadcast.

The range is limited and largely depends on distance, terrain, the antenna you're using, and the amount of power you put out.

Operate on a 'push to talk' framework; you cannot talk until the frequency is clear and the other person has finished transmitting. Unlike a normal phone call, this is not how we intuitively converse.

Proper long-distance broadcasting requires a license, which isn't expensive or difficult to obtain, but will require a written exam.

FRS radios

These walkie-talkies are affordable means for two-way communication over a limited range (a few miles at most). Some even allow digital transmission, meaning you can send text messages.

GMRS radios

These are also in the category of walkie-talkies but have more power and a greater range. In ideal conditions, you can get up to a couple of dozen miles of range.

CB radios

Citizen band radios are still used by truckers and can be plugged into a car. If you have one of these and are stuck on the interstate, you can almost always find out what the hold-up is. This is a low-power solution that is dependable for very localized two-way communication.

Amateur radio

Amateur radio, also known as ham radio, is for preppers who want to get serious about long-distance two-way communication. However, you need to be licensed to broadcast with these powerful and expensive radios. In the US, the FCC can fine you heavily for disrupting official broadcasting channels.

How to Protect Electronics From An EMP With A Faraday Cage

Difficulty: Easy

All electronics are susceptible to damage in the event of an electromagnetic pulse. If you're prepping for this scenario, you must protect your comms equipment.

To do this, you need to make a Faraday Cage. A faraday cage is an enclosed space with an electrically conductive material, such as metal, surrounding it. This cage blocks electromagnetic fields, such as radio waves, so the enclosed space is shielded from these fields. If you put your electronics in a faraday cage, the cage will block out the electromagnetic fields. This means that your electronics will not be able to receive or transmit signals.

Building a faraday cage is dead simple. If you have a metal box, then you're already done! Otherwise, you can put one together with mesh:

1. Find a box (wooden or cardboard) large enough to fit all your electronics.

2. Using a metal mesh screen or aluminum foil, wrap the entire box, including the lid.

3. Glue or tape the foil in place, making sure to cover the entire box.

4. Pay special attention to corners and edges. Any gap will allow electromagnetic radiation to leak through.

5. Place your electronics inside and close the lid.

6. Make sure the foil on the lid touches the foil on the sides of the box so it is connected.

7. Your electronics are now shielded from electromagnetic radiation!

(Now take them out, you probably want to use them)

The Bug-Out Bag List

A bug-out bag is a portable kit containing everything you need to survive if a situation forces you to evacuate immediately. Ideally, it's light enough to carry without burdening yourself but still contains the essentials you need to survive.

- ☐ Water – as much as you can carry without overburdening yourself.
- ☐ Food – lightweight non-perishables are the best.
- ☐ Protein bars
- ☐ MRE's
- ☐ Mini propane tank
- ☐ Knife
- ☐ Sleeping bag
- ☐ Torch
- ☐ First aid kit
- ☐ Medications
- ☐ Extra clothes
- ☐ Socks
- ☐ Underwear
- ☐ Thermal layers
- ☐ Hat with neck protection
- ☐ Rain poncho
- ☐ Sunscreen
- ☐ Cash
- ☐ Important documents
- ☐ Map
- ☐ Compass
- ☐ Radio
- ☐ Batteries
- ☐ Lighter / Matches
- ☐ Duct Tape (25')
- ☐ 55 Gal. Contractor Garbage Bag (Qty 2)
- ☐ Resealable Bags (Qty 5, Various Sizes)
- ☐ Sunglasses
- ☐ N95 Face Mask
- ☐ Whistle
- ☐ Pepper Spray and/or handgun
- ☐ Hand sanitizer
- ☐ Travel toothbrush & toothpaste
- ☐ Tissues

Emergency Organizations and Groups

United Kingdom

Local Emergency Management Agencies

- ☐ National emergency numbers: 999 / 112
- ☐ National Grid: 0800 6783 105 or 105 / 0800 40 40 90
- ☐ Department of Business, Energy and Industrial Strategy (BEIS): 0300 068 6900
- ☐ Gas Emergency Services: 0800 111 999
- ☐ UK Power Networks: 105/0800 31 63 105
- ☐ Northern Ireland Electricity Networks: 03457 643 643
- ☐ Electricity North West: 105 / 0800 195 4141
- ☐ SP Energy Networks: 0800 092 9290 / 0800 001 5400
- ☐ Scottish and Southern Electricity Networks: 105
- ☐ British Red Cross support line: 0808 196 3651
- ☐ National Health Service: 111
- ☐ Police line (non-emergency): 112

Community Services

- ☐ Association of Lowland Search & Rescue: 03333 129 999
- ☐ Anderby Volunteer Emergency Response Team (AVERT): 01522 552222
- ☐ Community Resilience North Somerset: 01934 888 888 / 07496 233001
- ☐ The Salvation Army: (020) 7367 4500
- ☐ Victim Support: 08 08 16 89 111
- ☐ Radio Amateurs Emergency Network (RAYNET): 0303 040 1080
- ☐ Royal Voluntary Service: 0330 555 0310

United States

Local Emergency Management Agencies

- National emergency number: 911
- American Red Cross: 1 800 RED CROSS (1-800-733-2767)
- Federal Emergency Management Agency (FEMA): 1-800-621-3362
- American Association of Poison Control Centers (AAPCC): 1-800-222-1222
- HHS – U.S. Department of Health and Human Services: 1-877-696-6775

Community Services

- The National Association for Amateur Radio (ARRL): 1-860-594-0200
- Americares Help Hotline: 1-203-658-9500
- AmeriCorps Hotline: 1-800-942-2677
- Direct Relief: 1-805-964-4767
- Headwaters Relief Organization: 763-233-7655
- REACT International: (866) 732-2899
- Team Rubicon: (310) 640-8787

Basic Safety Tips And Precautions

When working on DIY projects, remember that safety must always come first. There are a few simple steps you can take to protect yourself and those around you.

1. Wear the appropriate clothing and protective gear. This includes safety goggles, gloves, a dust mask, and ear protection. If possible, have a partner or a friend present when working with power tools.

2. Follow the instructions. Make sure you read the instructions thoroughly and understand the steps before you begin any project. This will help ensure you take the necessary safety precautions and have the right materials ready.

3. Secure your workspace. Make sure your workspace is free from clutter or debris and that any power cords are out of the way. Additionally, make sure you work when there's enough light so that you can clearly see what you are doing at all times.

4. Work with power tools correctly and safely. Be sure to read the instruction manual for the tool when it's your first time using it, and always wear the appropriate protective gear (can't stress this enough). Check for signs of damage on your machine before use; if it's damaged, don't plug it in. Unplug machines or power tools when not in use.

5. Keep all tools and materials in a safe place. If you have children or pets in the house, consider locking up your tools when not in use. Lastly, never take on a project or use any tools if you are tired, intoxicated, or under the influence of drugs.

It's Better with Friends!

Join our community on facebook
full of like-minded people living a
self-sufficient life.

Scan this QR Code:

Or go to:
facebook.com/groups/homesteadingforfunpeople

easygreenguides

Thanks for Reading

Please Leave a Review!

I would be *incredibly* appreciative if you could rate my book or leave a review on **Amazon**.

Your feedback helps me write better books.

Get Your Self-Sufficiency Checklist

It comes with:
- **A quickstart checklist** — Things that you can do almost immediately that will reduce your reliance on others.
- **A skills checklist** — Valuable skills that you should start learning yesterday!
- **And more** in-depth checklists about topics such as: food, water, energy, waste management, and more.

To get it for free, visit:

www.easygreenguides.com/checklist

A complete bibliography is available online at:

easygreenguides.com/nogridbibliography